WELCOME TO EARTH

A Guide for Walk-ins, Starseeds and Lightworkers of All Varieties

Hannah Beaconsfield

Welcome to Earth

ISBN 0-929385-98-5

Published by
Light Technology Publishing
P.O. Box 1526
Sedona, AZ 86339
1-800-450-0985

Printed by
MISSION POSSIBLE
Commercial Printing
P.O. Box 1495
Sedona, AZ 86339

ACKNOWLEDGMENTS

I'd like to thank the following people: Dorothy Bates, for her editorial expertise and repeated, patient proofreading; Nina and Peter Van Moorsel, for their multilevel support; Lyssa Royal-Holt, for her gifts as a channeling teacher; and Dr. Julie Pierce for anchoring the project on this plane.

Welcome to Earth

Contents

PART 3
EXTRATERRESTRIAL CONNECTIONS

PART 4

FINALE

FOREWORD

LIZ NELSON

What Is a Walk-in?

As founder of WE (Walk-ins for Evolution) International, an organization connecting walk-ins around the world, and as editor of the WE newsletter, I have long awaited a book such as *Welcome to Earth: A Guide for Walk-ins, Starseeds and Lightworkers of All Varieties.* Aside from a few books that relate the story of a specific walk-in life, there has been nothing as comprehensive, helpful, informative and clear since the world of walk-ins was first brought to our attention by best-selling author Ruth Montgomery.

In her 1979 groundbreaking book *Strangers Among Us*, Montgomery introduced us to that little-known or -understood phenomenon called the "walk-in." She stated, "Walk-ins are beings who have attained sufficient awareness of the meaning of life so they can forego the process of birth and childhood to return to Earth directly to adult bodies." She claimed that walk-ins have been coming by the tens of thousands, each with a service or mission of use to humanity. And it's not a new phenomenon, she assured us: Jesus Christ, Benjamin Franklin, Abraham Lincoln — and more recently, Anwar Sadat — were all walk-ins. In 1986 she featured several walk-ins under her title *Threshold to Tomorrow.* And in 1983 Carol Parrish, named a walk-in by Montgomery, gave us *Messengers of Hope.* The three books are classics on walk-in information.

Montgomery and Parrish define this phenomenon as an exchange of souls in a physical body. The replacement can take place at any time and under any circumstance. Many souls choose to walk in during a near-death experience, an accident, a suicide attempt, a serious illness or simply during a quiet interlude. Accidents, sometimes followed by a coma, account for a good number of soul exchanges. The reason for this seems to be that the conscious mind, whose job it is to protect the physical being, is rendered unconscious at such times and the exchange can be made without its interference.

Four years ago, about nine years after I "walked in," I started the WE newsletter because I simply knew it was time for walk-ins to connect in order to hasten our work. WE International has uncovered new information that suggests the term *walk-in* might need to be changed or at least broadened. Before I came to know so many walk-ins, my definition was fairly simple and straightforward: a walk-in is a soul who is invited to complete a life in progress by a soul who wants out or is simply done with the life. This exchange is always for a specific humanitarian purpose and is never forced.

While that definition still rings true, some say their host soul never "walked out" or that the one who walked in was not a different soul, but merely a higher aspect of their own oversoul coming to begin service. Others say they are sharing a body with an other-dimension being who is wiser, more spiritual, can see the overall picture and guide the work to be done. And still others say their bodies have been host to several soul exchanges, each completing a task and taking the consciousness higher.

To complicate matters further, WE has detected five types or categories of walk-ins. These categories are based on the "home base," source or vibration of the walk-ins. Their points of origin are:

- Hierarchic vibration (Christian, Buddhist)
- Interplanetary alliances (Pleiades, Arcturus, Sirius)
- Group-soul vibrations (oversoul, master soul, family soul)
- Universal vibrations (spirit, creative energy, universal mind)
- Angelic realm beings.

There is often overlapping. A group-soul walk-in might talk about a Christ consciousness and an interplanetary walk-in might embrace the concept of creative energy. But no matter where they're from, whether there is a merging or an actual exchange, the soul is in for a great deal of change, turmoil and confusion.

Part of the confusion stems from the fact that in most cases the entering has not been conscious. The soul needs to ground itself into the body, mind and emotional natures, much to the bewilderment of the conscious mind. In a way, it's very much like moving into an old house but not remembering why. Nevertheless, you begin to rewire, paint, add or knock down walls, replace the heating system and add new furniture and carpeting to make the house livable again.

When you redecorate a room, it takes forethought, time and energy. From stripping the wallpaper to cleaning up and repositioning furniture, you don't expect to change the room overnight. And that's redecorating only one room. Think in terms of redecorating a whole house, and the magnitude of "redecorating" a life — body, mind and soul — begins to sink in.

All of it takes time and hard work. In the past, the period needed for integration and grounding of the new soul or soul combination into the body has been between nine and twelve years, because most walk-ins had to function with very little help and had almost no contact with each other.

WE International has largely changed that situation by serving as a vehicle that enables walk-ins to get to know one another, assist each other through the process, grow together, exchange information and accelerate their work. WE has also found that although walk-ins do enter to accomplish a particular mission or work, that work isn't necessarily something tangible, such as teaching or healing. Some say they are in various parts of the world simply to anchor the intensified energies now coming to our planet.

Detractors of the idea that walk-ins are a reality claim that the universe doesn't allow one soul to take over the karma of another, and they're right. What they fail to distinguish, though, is the difference between responsibility (children, for instance) and karma. Walk-ins do assume the responsibilities that the host soul set in motion, and part of the bargain is that they must see them through to the best of their ability. It's the price they pay for the opportunity for personal growth and service; to them, it seems a fair exchange.

There appears to be a sort of glamour surrounding the phenomenon. Sometimes people wistfully say to me that they wish they were a walk-in. Actually, one of the things plaguing the walk-ins Ruth Montgomery named in *Threshold to Tomorrow* was that people expected them to be perfect, putting them on a pedestal. Nothing could be further from the truth. Walk-ins come in just as many shapes, sizes, mentalities and ego temperaments as those who are born into a physical body. They have past-life issues and need to grow in awareness just as anyone else does.

The only differences I've been able to discern, once walk-ins come into their own spiritual power, are:

1. Their specific work, service or mission becomes an almost obsessive focus.

2. Their outlook tends to be more universal/humanitarian.

3. Since they're newly entered from the spiritual realm, they bring with them — or maybe they just remember more clearly — certain spiritual abilities that everyone has, but has forgotten in the years since birth.

In the end, the greatest work of all walk-ins might be merely to remind everyone to find their own inner spiritual power and to use it now.

As I write this, WE is going into its fourth year. I would never have believed in the begining that WE would, in its first year (and as a result of the first conference for walk-ins in 1994) expand from a fledgling quarterly newsletter to the official publication for the then-newly formed walk-in organization, WE International. Or that in its second year Ruth Montgomery would attend the second national conference, and walk-ins from seventeen states would pay tribute to her at a banquet held in her honor. Or that in its third year WE would hold regional conferences in Tacoma, Washington; Springfield, Missouri; and St. Paul, Minnesota. Or that in its fourth year now, WE would launch the New Awareness Speakers Bureau to bring soft spirituality to the workplace, colleges and university campuses and would plan to hold a Healing the Walk-in Workshop in St. Paul, a last regional conference in Philadelphia, Pennsylvania, and another national gathering in St. Paul — this one honoring Carol Parrish and Ed Hager for their service to humanity. If you had told me in 1994 that all of this would occur, I simply wouldn't have believed you. But I assure you (and myself at times) that this and more has indeed happened.

Belief is an elusive thing. What you believe today can change radically tomorrow or even in the next moment. As you read *Welcome to Earth,* I urge you to do it from the inside out. You don't have to believe everything you read, but if something resonates for you or within you, see how it fits. Keep what you need and let the rest go.

Spiritual transformation, whether or not you're a walk-in, is one of the most exciting adventures you will ever experience, though it sometimes feels hazardous. Hannah Beaconsfield, in this fine book, has tried to make it as safe and painless as possible.

February 1997

Welcome to Earth

INTRODUCTION

In September 1996 I received channeled information that there would be a large influx of walk-in spirits moving onto the Earth plane in the next few years. They will be coming in large numbers to assist with the accelerating transformation of this world as we approach the end of the century.

My guides, the Pleiadian Light, asked that I put a book together from articles I had already published. They said the new walk-ins were going to need a lot of sources of information to help them orient to this world.

My initial reaction was to assist anonymously, because there is too much baggage attached to the idea of walk-ins. They told me that I wouldn't need to be anonymous if I presented the information properly. They said I should stress that walk-ins really need help adjusting to the lives they take on and should not be regarded as something special or unusual to be either admired or ridiculed.

Whatever way we arrive on this plane, once we are here we are all playing the same game. There are both advantages and disadvantages to either group — being born into the bodies we use or walking in and bypassing the conditioning of childhood.

The guides who are the primary source of information in this book are two different energies. *The Pleiadian Light* is extraterrestrial energy, which represents the Pleiadian culture from their position as an integrated light source. (We are moving toward this same integration and the Pleiadians wish to help us with our progress.) *Grace* is the interdimensional energy who defines herself as a representation of the Christ consciousness through a female-archetype energy.

There is another guide source included in this book: *White Crow*. She is a former incarnation of mine, a Native American medicine woman. She is from a time period long antedating any of the historically known tribes.

Many of the articles in this book were originally published

in the *Walk-ins for Evolution* newsletter and *The Lantern*, a newsletter that I publish. I have retained the format of articles on different subjects for this book, grouping them according to similarity of subject matter. My guides have channeled some new material to tie this information together.

Though the book was "requested" to assist new walk-in spirits, much of the information is generic metaphysical guidance and helpful to all as we go through transformations and enter a new millennium.

Hannah Beaconsfield
New York, New York
December 31, 1996

Part 1

The Walk-in Process

ONE

Channeling

Grace

We introduce ourselves as Christ consciousness integrating female-archetype energy. We have had many names in many cultures on your plane. Through this channel we choose to call ourselves Grace.

Our energy is the quality of mercy. We represent the benevolence of loving, accepting and allowing. Ours is the energy that forgives all debts, for we understand that your indebtedness is to your learning processes, which have no reality on our plane. Our energy loves your plane and exists to support it. We send our greeting at this time to assure all who are undertaking the great drama of life on your world that you are not alone in your struggles. You are loved and regarded with admiration for the challenges you have undertaken.

Earth is a playground for tightly focused games where there is little awareness of the realities that lie beyond it. The rules of the game were chosen as a challenge and an opportunity for the growth of the souls who have taken up lifetimes here. As in your game blindman's buff, handicaps were selected to allow concentration on the development of other soul characteristics.

The primary illusion of the Earth plane is that it is alone in the universe — that this, except for some vague idea of an afterlife, is all there is. The blindfold game has served its purpose, and it is time to allow your perceptions of reality to expand. The Earth experience of isolation and detachment from the center of all energy or God has been taken to the maximum level of value. The process of opening your eyes to the many worlds beyond yours is under way.

Understand that your world is entering the age of light. Light or positivity will not vanquish darkness or negativity, but the negative aspects will integrate with the energies of light, for they are portions of the God source, too.

The channeling process, as it is presently occurring on your plane, is a means by which other dimensions of reality interact with yours. The virtual explosion of channeled information now coming through to your world is in preparation for the age of light and the alterations in your perceptual abilities. There are two main sources of the information being transmitted to your plane: One is extraterrestrial civilizations who wish to make contact now that you are opening to other realities; the other is interdimensional energies like ours, who are drawn to assist you in understanding the changes taking place.

The people who are channels for this communication are like telephones between various worlds. History has always had oracles, mediums and channels, but never in the number that are presently opening to this ability. In the past, the person bringing through the material was often in so deep a trance as to be unconscious of the event. This is often called full-body channeling. At the present time most of those awakening to the channeling process are semitrance channels who have a conscious awareness of what is being communicated, though they are in a detached, altered state. Often these channels do not remember the details of what has been said until they listen to the tape or read a transcription of their channeling.

It is very important that there be open consciousness in the process, because the input from the Earth-focused consciousness colors the material for better understanding by others with the same kinship. It is also because semiconscious channeling is a bridge to the next step — conscious channeling.

Conscious channeling necessitates an almost imperceptible shift in pulling in data from an outside source and commenting by the living-plane consciousness of the individual. This ability is what your mass consciousness is moving toward. Eventually this type of data access will be natural for everyone.

The channels of today are like the historical scribes — a gifted and educated few who could read and write. Living in an educated country, your current population is almost all literate. This is also how it will be in your future in relation to channelling. Easy interaction with other physical worlds and other dimensions will be commonplace.

For now, we communicate through your scribes to guide and teach you expanded vision as you are removing your blindfolds and revealing your true capabilities and unlimited dimensions.

Sometimes people ask why different channels bring through seemingly contradictory explanations for the same information. Understand that there is a massive amount of channeled data and no one can have the whole truth. Each channel has a piece of a mosaic that will ultimately create a magnificent picture. Each channel's piece is colored to catch the attention of beings who will be most intrigued and excited by that information. In other words, channels offer the material in the most accessible form for those who are on the same wavelength.

The different entities coming through channels also produce different types of data. The ET communicators are sending information about their civilizations, histories, perceptions of reality and relationships with God. The interdimensional beings are assisting and guiding those on Earth through the turbulent waters of the present transformation. As vistas open that were never part of the beliefs or realities of a civilization, there can be some disorientation, fear or confusion. There can be a sense of imbalance at the loss of the dimensions of reality that had been relied upon.

It is our desire to always be available and to support your intellectual understanding and your emotional stability as the age of light reveals the greatly expanded parameters of your reality.

Whether you seek channeled information or address us directly, know that we are here. We hear you and we send energies of loving support to assist you on your journey out of darkness into the age of light.

TWO

Defining Walk-ins, Starseeds and Lightworkers

For a phenomenon that is very complex, I feel that the concept of walk-ins is sketchy at best. The true nature and extent of consciousness is not available through the human mechanism that is our vehicle for perception. Therefore, we must construct concepts that come as close to reality as our limited consciousness can accommodate.

Walk-ins share more than one spirit energy operating through one physical vehicle. This can be accomplished in many ways. One spirit can replace another, though the vehicle will always carry programming from the original spirit. Replacements can be gradual, with the incoming and outgoing spirits alternating in the body for a period of time. Split-second replacements usually occur in the case of a traumatic incident such as an accident. Many near-death experiences involve walk-in situations. There are also situations in which the spirit energy blends or braids into the original spirit; they then vibrate as a single spirit energy.

I feel most walk-in situations are between soul-family members, which means they are compatible and even familiar with each other. I know there are situations in which a spirit with no family connections takes on an "abandoned" body. Urgent need can make this type of exchange necessary. This situation can cause severe, even psychotic disorientation and a particularly painful adjustment period.

I'm sure there are many more variations of this process. But I also think the process itself is getting too much attention. It is more important to focus on why this phenomenon is happening in such numbers at this time, what purpose the walk-ins have come to serve and what help they can be given.

Starseeds are spirits whose connections and experiences are primarily with an extraterrestrial civilization. They have little or no experience with Earth life, and they come into this world with the birth of the body. In some ways starseeds have a more difficult time than walk-ins because from the beginning they often feel out of sync with society and their parents. They can carry this sense of being an outsider throughout their lives. However, many starseeds meet and create an insular group or partner relationship in which they establish their own world consciousness, thereby gaining a sense of peace and belonging.

Everyone on Earth is, at the most intrinsic level, a lightworker. However, this term usually refers to those who are actively working toward the transformation of this world to an integrated energy unit that radiates light, not darkness. When we say "actively working," we don't mean just being conscious of the work they are doing, for many lightworkers are active when they are on the dream plane. Eventually, all Earth personnel will be active lightworkers. The Earth is giving birth to a new version of herself and there are millions of midwives assisting.

THREE

A Theater Piece

The Saga of Three Walk-in Generations

Blythe

I am a walk-in to this body and this life. I'm not the body's first, but its second spirit replacement, which makes me the third spirit occupant, counting the one born into the body. This is not an unusual phenomenon. I will not be this body's last walk-in either. After that it is open-ended, depending on the world situation and what is needed. This circumstance, when measured against Earth history, is appropriate for the current world situation.

I prefer the term "spirit replacement." However, I recognize that "walk-in" is a commonly recognized term. I equate the walk-in phenomenon with the situation you find in a long-running Broadway show, in which the leading actors play out their contracts and are then replaced by other actors. The new actors bring their particular qualities to the roles and there are some changes, but the show goes on. This is a limited analogy, but it does cast some light on a difficult concept.

The first walk-in to this body arrived in 1982. The original occupant was called Ann. The spirit replacement was a future extraterrestrial incarnation of the original personality and a counterpart of mine as well. She was a Pleiadian called Spandia from about four hundred years in the future. At the time of the first walk-in, a decision was made to take on a new professional name — Hannah Beaconsfield. I have come to understand that this is an umbrella name for several entities.

Ann's life had reached a point where she had accomplished all she could, given her resources for that lifetime. She had lost everything of any value to her: career, marriage and friends. There was nothing to hold her here, and she had a standing agreement, entered into before her birth, to make the vehicle available for service as the age of light approached.

Originally the project was for a walk-in to remain for the duration of the life. However, after the Harmonic Convergence in 1987 there was a shift and an acceleration of the world potential. It became possible to bring in much more energy, so a changing of the guard was possible.

My perception of the walk-in process involves an awareness that the living-plane consciousness, which interacts in everyday life, remains after the spirit replacement comes in. I refer to this portion of consciousness as *the caretaker*. I feel it is an extension of consciousness by the physical aspect into the social structure of the life. It is a constant that is then woven into the fabric of the new spirit's life. At the same time, the new spirit begins to make changes in the caretaker to bring it more in line with its own characteristics.

This caretaker is both a boon and a bane. On one hand, the new spirit is initially dependent upon this aspect to guide it in personal life situations and social interactions in this world. On the other hand, this aspect has been conditioned with all sorts of distortions, illusions, dysfunctions and life baggage. These obstacles must be removed before the walk-in can work effectively. This period of adjustment can sometimes feel as though the blind is leading the crippled. This is not easy. It could proceed more comfortably with support from people who are part of the walk-in's life situation and/or a therapist who is open-minded regarding the phenomenon.

Ideas have been disseminated that walk-ins are highly skilled, superior beings who are here to set the Earth straight. This does a disservice to spirits struggling valiantly to adjust to an unfamiliar world. Walk-ins might have some skills that are different from Earth folk, but they are equal spirits come to lend a hand at this momentous time in Earth's evolution.

When Spandia replaced Ann in 1982, the living-plane consciousness was not aware what was happening. She was confused, because some days she felt positive and harmonious, yet overnight she would sink into deep depression. Ann and Spandia alternated in the body for a period of time to give both a chance to make adjustments. Though Ann had studied metaphysics for many years, she could not have conceived of the drama that was unfolding without being led to information that described it.

She found needed information in Ruth Montgomery's book *Strangers Among Us.* Once Ann had the concept, there was a strong sense that this phenomenon was happening to her. However, there was no community support for her. She was very much alone with many doubts. In an effort to gain verification, she wrote to Ruth Montgomery.

Ms. Montgomery replied with a form letter stating that she had so many requests that her guides were no longer identifying walk-ins. But she penned a note at the bottom saying that it definitely sounded like a walk-in situation to her. It was just a few words, but they meant so much! (It is important that the walk-in get some sort of feedback and support.)

Spandia eventually took over the body and the life circumstances. Part of her agenda was to experience the rich and varied emotions that are part of the Earth's polarities. Pleiadians long ago chose to forgo the emotions we consider negative. As a Pleiadian creative artist, she took these emotional experiences back home via her art. This vicariously served to expand the consciousness of her culture.

Before other work could begin, the difficult Earth situation she took over required her to dedicate the first few years entirely to healing the life. Channeling and easy access to other-life recall were skills she brought in. She had the good fortune to find a therapist in a conventional medical situation who had the courage to allow her to pursue reincarnational therapy and speak freely as a replacement spirit. But Spandia also escalated the life drama to soap-opera proportions for the purpose of exploring emotions. (Some of that mess she left for me to clean up.)

Spandia was in the body from 1982 to 1992. Her agenda was to bring in healing for the life and to set up skills that would assist those who followed her in residence here. These skills were to provide a basis for active support of the changes in Earth consciousness, which is moving into the age of light.

I walked into the body in July 1992. I am a future extraterrestrial energy, too. My culture is Essassani and we are one of the hybrid races created by the blending of Earth and Zeta Reticuli genetics. (The image of short, large-headed and big-eyed ETs described in contact encounters are Zetas.) This hybrid project is still current. One of my reasons for walking in is to participate in this project. In a sense, I am working to ensure the evolution of my own future reality. You see, we come to serve our worlds *and* this one.

One of my projects is to help defuse the abduction fears rampant in the UFO community. All participants in contact scenarios have agreed on a spirit level to assist in these interworld actions. Most participants have future incarnations as the hybrids they are helping to create. Personally, Earth is my ancient home and I carry a deep sensitivity for this magnificent world, its people and history.

My culture communicates telepathically, so beings do not have names. We recognize each other by what you might call a *thought tone*. To identify my energy, I chose the name "Blythe." I used this when channeling through this vehicle before I walked in.

Other vehicles who are experiencing a series of spirit replacements have chosen to change names with each new entrant. This is valuable in establishing and stabilizing the new identity quickly, but it depends on where they are working and the people with whom they interact. My umbrella name is better suited to the territory in which I find myself.

Before I took over the body, I channeled that preparations were under way for an exchange to take place, so the caretaker consciousness was forewarned. Even so, the adjustments have been almost unbearable. If I hadn't been able to channel guidance, I might have gone totally mad.

I know what talents, experiences and resources I have available to me. Some I'm bringing into the life; some were left in the programming by Ann and Spandia. I don't know yet how I will orchestrate these abilities. Ann's profession was dance, so I have her education and experience available to choreograph and teach dance. Spandia is a Pleiadian "thought artist" with the capacity to project thought images on a sensitized surface or in holographic form. She brought in skills that translate to drawing and painting on this plane. Shortly after she walked in, she entered art classes and was soon using the skills to earn a living.

I, Blythe, bring in skills as a drummer. Within a few weeks after walking in I saw a woman playing a frame drum and felt compelled to learn it. I have channeled through drumming skills very quickly, to the chagrin of the caretaker; this part is still trying to tell me that I have no talent in this area, so why am I pursuing it?

On my world drumming is a powerful form of expression. Being telepathic means that we do not have vocal expression. However, our genetic connections with Earth life and the brilliant levels of vocal accomplishment here give us an impulse to make communicative sounds. Drumming is our voice and is used more like singing than a spoken message, with tonal melodies blended with the beats.

My work at home is as a community ceremonial facilitator and leader — a translation might be a "choreographer who stages communal events." There really isn't anything quite like it on Earth, because the Essassani operate as a very cohesive society. These events include social and spiritual elements and are a natural forum for us.

Earth consciousness creates a challenge for incoming spirits because it is separated into compartments; this is a world of specialists. In one individual there are physical, emotional, mental and spiritual bodies of consciousness. Also, the psyche is divided into the id, ego and superego. There are still other separate states of consciousness associated with different brain-wave activities: alpha, beta, theta, delta. All of these compartments handle different aspects of the individual, and although they interact, they do not truly integrate. Many walk-ins come from realities in which not only the individual consciousness but the social structure of the culture is highly integrated. This is a major adjustment for some walk-ins.

Speaking from the position of a caretaker who has observed two spirit replacements, I can say with certainty that each walk-in scenario is different. The variables include the life situation of the original spirit, the source of the incoming spirit and the fact that the entire Earth population is going through a transformation — which is difficult enough without the walk-in scenario. In addition, consciousness and reality are much more fluid and malleable than this world has ever considered. Thus there are many variations on the walk-in phenomenon.

This is a unique time on Earth and many are taking advantage of the growth service opportunities here. My adventure is just beginning. I feel like I'm waiting in a theater for the curtain to go up. God, I hope this time it's a musical comedy!

The Saga Continues

Kristan

Blythe's dream of having a musical comedy life was not realized. I am the spirit replacement who has followed her — number four. I identify myself by the name Kristan and I expect to be here for quite a while.

Blythe's experience is a good example of how fast this world is changing and how difficult it is to take over an Earth life. Blythe walked into the life with the intention of spending roughly ten years, equal to Spandia's tenure. Her agenda involved opening an awareness of the intergalactic community that surrounds this world and helping prepare for open interactions with otherworld cultures. Her channeling contributed to this, but her presence especially helped create a reassuring feeling about extraterrestrials in her living area simply by her being there.

Probabilities allow for the potential of the same goals to be achieved in a variety of ways. Those unfamiliar with the concept must understand that all variations of any given event play out in the multidimensional levels of reality. However, Earth is limited by the illusion of linear time and therefore can only experience one line of reality.

During stable times in this world's history there has been a long-term steady flow along a single line of probability. A shift to another probability usually occurred when an accumulation of energy for change supported it. The present magnitude of energy for change is causing many shifts in probabilities. Many elements of the present reality are changing, and shifting surges of energy can make today's probable line of development obsolete tomorrow.

Blythe's time in residence was cut short because some expected developments got lost in the probabilities. The anticipated walk-in of her Essassani mate, who was to be her partner on this plane, did not occur because changes in the intended vehicle made it unsuitable.

Her own qualities were ill-suited to working here without the support of a partner. The choice of the name Blythe gives some indication of her nature. She had a light, fairylike quality; she was never really comfortable in the harsh realities of New York City. The nonverbal aspect of the Essassani culture also translated to difficulty in using her voice here. She felt very handicapped in this area, adding to the other pressures.

In fact, we almost lost the body during her time in residence. The stress of a new energy altering the body, along with the expansion of the energy of the throat chakra involved in channeling, unbalanced the thyroid. Her body weight dropped below one hundred pounds, electrolytes were unbalanced and necessary nutrients were lost.

During one warm, humid night in Central Park, Blythe joined in a folk dance and tried to dance at a level the body once knew. In the middle of dancing she felt deeply exhausted. Thinking she was going to die, she had to sit down. Only in retrospect did she recognize that cardiac arrest had been a real possibility. Many guides rushed to her assistance, but it was apparent Earth life was much more difficult than had been anticipated.

An additional reason for Blythe's difficulties had to do with the way she chose to project her spirit to this time and place. She left her Essassani body in suspended animation for the time she was working on Earth. She was focused here with mostly channeled support from home.

Spandia, by contrast, operated on this plane when she was asleep on her own world. When she was asleep on Earth she went home to her Pleiadian body and was awake and active in that world. This allowed her to handle more difficult circumstances because she went home every day for rebalancing and guidance.

However, in the three years that Blythe was here, she managed to accomplish all the things she had intended to do. One important reason for her opting for time on Earth was to gain a firsthand experience communicating on this world in order to improve channeled communications from the Essassani culture to this plane.

The Essassani, despite the absence of a spoken language, are great intergalactic communicators. In their channeled communications with Earth they use computer-assisted language translation. It was felt that some of these communications lacked subtle sensitivities to Earth emotions and that firsthand experiences could adjust the computer programming.

Blythe obtained ample experience to take back to her world. One of the most painful aspects of Earth life for her was how isolated each individual is. Even those with close families are isolated in their individuality. This is different from the Essassani culture where everyone is linked by empathy, telepathy and a strong sense of unity and community. You can see why, without a close partner, she couldn't stay in this world for too long.

Her agenda was nevertheless fulfilled because she brought drumming for the use of the vehicle's total life. She initiated the publication of the newsletter *The Lantern*, which set in motion energies designed to support peaceful contact with other worlds. She acquired emotional experience while on Earth to ensure clearer communications between her civilization and this one in future channeling and, eventually, in open contact. It might not have been a musical comedy production, but her soul family gives a bravo! for her performance.

I, Kristan, was prepared to move in sooner than had been anticipated. However, the body was not fully prepared to receive my level of energy. (Sounds like another soap opera, doesn't it?) I came into the body as a spirit replacement on August 20, 1995.

The first year was another period of severe adjustment. My energy might never be able to operate fully through a physical vehicle. I am fortunate to have a caretaker consciousness who is aware of the process and has sufficient metaphysical understanding to captain the ship as I gradually move my energy into a control position.

My spirit is not a projection from an ET culture. My energy is interdimensional and its source is the future — a future in which the integration of the Earth energies into a planet of light has already occurred. In a sense, I've projected an individualized energy unit backward to ensure that the integration to a planetary consciousness of light is on the highest energy line of probability.

Even though I represent Earth energy, in some ways I feel more alien than the ET walk-ins who preceded me in this body. They still retained the sense of being part of a physical world culture, though translations occurred to assist accommodation. In many ways my energy is further removed. Coming from a consciousness level that is totally integrated, I sometimes feel lost in the incredible spectrum of emotions in this world. Sometimes I'm operating from an overview that might appear to be coolly detached to those who are deeply entrenched in Earth emotions. It is not true that I don't perceive the pain. I am *very* sensitive to what is going on.

When I allow myself to dip into the whirlpool of emotions, I often feel too sensitive to handle the present level of polarity. I have to withdraw, not listen to news or see any movies or TV shows that are serving to purge the Earth's levels of negative impulses. I find them almost impossible to handle.

However, I am learning to juggle the various levels of consciousness and the wide spectrum of expressions of those levels. With the help of the caretaker consciousness, I am learning to function on this plane and bring in the energy I will need for my agenda here. The skills I have been adding to this individualized Earth stew are an expansion of communication through writing, and organization and integration of the different talents and experiences that have been brought into this body/life by my predecessors. I will use these skills in my support of the transformation of this planet, which for me resonates as home.

The walk-ins, starseeds and lightworkers on this plane are caught in many of the same difficulties that I am. We will move beyond the adjustments by assisting one another. We share the same long-range goal — to see this incredible world evolve to a beacon of integrated energy shining as a brilliant light source in the omniverse.

FOUR

Challenges in the Walk-in Processes

The Pleiadian Light

Walking into the Maelstrom

Most walk-ins prepare to move onto the Earth plane with the confidence that they can deal with the Earth reality competently; and they can. However, once operating through an Earth body in the structure of this world's psyche, things look different. To various degrees, the spirit replacement experiences some of the "forgetfulness" that is part of being born on this plane.

Those who are completely aware of who they are and why they are here, as well as those who haven't a clue that anything has changed, have it easier than those in the gray areas between. The disorientation that occurs when you are perceiving two realities and trying to integrate them into a single living experience can be very disturbing.

Earth operates at a high level of fear. This energy generates the growth of a 3D civilization. Competition for survival feeds on fear for energy. This is true on the most primitive level as well as on present levels of technological development. It is such a pervasive energy that its more subtle aspects go unrecognized or are considered normal. For Earth, fear is the norm.

Most spirits who are committed to serving the evolution of humanity by taking over a vehicle and a life, come from dimensions or otherworld cultures that are not driven by fear. The spirit replacements who find themselves in this maelstrom can experience a great deal of disorientation and pain; even low-grade fear can be felt as panic.

One thing a walk-in can do to handle this situation is recognize that fear generates energy, and energy must flow and move. When dammed, it grows in power. Allowing it to flow through you or giving it expression through movement is helpful.

In some cases a biochemical formula has been established by the preceding spirit that locks the body into a pattern of chemically initiated fear responses. Herbal remedies or medications are useful in breaking this pattern as long as an outlet for the energy is also maintained.

The most important thing to remember is that before you walked in, you had all the skills necessary to handle this world. Take advantage of any help available. Trust your own impulses and intuition in healing your Earth vehicle and its various bodies of consciousness.

Bridging the Void

During the walk-in's transitional or adjustment period there is a point at which the majority of the accouterments of the original occupant have been cleared out. The replacement spirit cannot fully establish his/her contributions to the life situation until this releasing is accomplished. Even though there is a blending of releasing and establishing, there is a period in the middle when you can feel as though you are in a void — not quite one thing or the other.

If you have taken over a life that has few close connections, this phase can be particularly disorienting; you might feel untethered and unstable. If you judge this state, you will create emotional reactions of desolation, depression and fear that add to the pain.

Even after a walk-in exchange has taken place, there is always a portion of the original consciousness that remains. This is the portion most closely connected to handling the mundane interactions necessary in a socially structured world such as yours. We often refer to this constant life monitor as the receptionist, the doorman or (as detailed in chapter 3) the caretaker.

The painful point in this exchange is when the incoming spirit is still feeling alien and the caretaker also feels alienated from many of the world associations that were familiar and comfortable. This situation is like someone buying out a company and instituting changes in company policy. The employees from the old guard who remain can feel very insecure and anxious until they accommodate the new owners.

In addition, much of the baggage of the original occupant had created painful life situations that were not only deemed negative, but probably contributed to the person's wish to leave. The mere absence of these negative aspects is read as progress. However, when there is a spirit replacement, changes take place in many positive personal aspects such as the preferences, skills and interests of the original occupant, and these changes can be read as losses for the caretaker.

This sense of loss creates a mourning response, and when the mourning is for loss of self, the caretaker can misinterpret the process. As an ending is anticipated, death thoughts can arise. You might say to yourself, "This certainly feels a lot like depression. Am I losing ground?"

We are going to have to ask you to *trust*. Trust that you are in a transitional situation and that what feels like emptiness is simply making room for the new qualities, skills and preferences that are being brought into the life. It is like entering a newly purchased empty house that appears bleak because all the former owner's furniture is gone. But you have a wonderful power tool in your world — imagination. You can use it to plan how you will decorate the house with your furnishings. It wouldn't enter your mind in this situation that there is something wrong and you will never move in your own furniture. Allowing for emptiness can allow for future fullness.

We are aware of how complex the nature of consciousness seems to be when you enter this world of limitation. However, many walk-ins have taken up Earth residence for the very purpose of expanding the restraints of limitation. As you figure out how to solve the problems of your adjustments, you are contributing knowledge that will expand the limits of the mass consciousness on Earth simply by being part of it.

Shattering Patterns and Getting Out of the Way

Change is change. That seems like an obvious statement, but the caretaker of the original life and body of a walk-in often tries desperately to maintain the status quo or return to "normal" in order to stabilize the life situation for the replacement spirit. Caretakers seem determined to prevent change. This portion of the consciousness is a maintainer of patterns.

There comes a time in the adjustment period when the walk-in spirit is present enough to take a dominant position. It must reach this position in order to implement the skills and take action to fulfill its agenda. If the caretaker is frightened of letting go, this conflict will add another dimension of stress to an already difficult situation. Sometimes the caretaker can be gently guided to release patterns that no longer serve the life. Other times the patterns have to be shattered in ways that are more aggressive.

Each replacement scenario will address this situation within the available dynamics. Some dramatic shattering of patterns can include the loss of home and possessions by natural disaster or fire. Accidents and unusual illnesses definitely break patterns in a forceful way. Death can take family and friends with a finality that opens the life to new patterns. In the case of personalities not given to that type of aggressive pattern-breaking, a period of withdrawal, isolation and removal from society can sever connections with past-life patterning just as effectively. This is a gentler method but might be intolerable for those who like action. These are extreme examples. It is more likely that moderate variations or combinations of these methods would be chosen for making necessary changes.

The most important help the caretaker can give at this point is to get out of the way, so we will address the concerns of the caretaker by giving suggestions for easing out of the way and feeling more comfortable about it.

Many of the problems that walk-ins complain about come from the caretaker level of consciousness. The caretaker needs to reassure him or herself regularly that a replacement has taken place and that he/she can help the incoming spirit by making affirmations that allow the replacement to take more and more control of the life. The caretaker also needs to remind herself to listen for guidance from the incoming spirit. The caretaker has an important role, but it is in service to the spirit. When the spirit and caretaker can blend and operate in a balanced, integrated way, the period of adjustment will have served its purpose.

We understand this is not easy to do. The Earth world and its perceptions of reality are based on beliefs that are carved in stone. It is a huge challenge to face a stone wall and say, "You are an illusion," and although you recognize that you are correct, you must not drive your car into that wall. That's metaphysics. The metaphysician is one who is comfortable with paradox. All is; that's all there is.

After the incoming spirit is integrated into the life, even more pattern-shattering might take place. The new walk-in might not feel aligned or even comfortable with some of the friends and associates of the original spirit. The integrated consciousness is faced with having to sever some connections with people and life situations that require a level of tact that would try an angelic being. In addition, there are often conflicts about whether these connections need to be cut at all. After all, there doesn't seem to be any harm in the connections; they've just become empty.

Each time the seasons change, patterns are shattered. Some flowers must die; they cannot be carried into the next season. Nature doesn't feel guilty. It simply moves ahead.

Remember, a replacement spirit has an alignment with the original resident, but by necessity it is sufficiently different to change the life — people left behind and old patterns released — even though there can be a lot of pain in the process. On the brighter side, when the caretaker lets go and gets out of the way, there might be a wonderful surge of energy and relief that propels forward the exchange process.

Rage of the Caged

There is a form of rage particular to walk-ins. The spirits who replace departing Earth souls can initially feel trapped, which adds to whatever challenges they have already taken on. In fact, given the extent of the difficulties involved in a spirit replacement, it is no wonder that a massive increase in this phenomenon is undertaken only when the need is so great that those who volunteer are willing to face the risks involved.

Replacement spirits come from worlds that do not have the limitations or the illusions that are part of the present Earth game plan. For some, entry onto this plane feels so restrictive that their reaction is translated into rage.

The situation is similar to when wild animals are placed in a zoo. The adjustment, no matter how well they are fed and cared for, can be overwhelming. The polar bears in the Central Park Zoo in New York City display neurotic repetitive behavior patterns. They even have their own animal psychologists (who, by the way, recommended more toys for them to play with).

The massive number of spirit replacements at this time could definitely use some psychologists of their own. More therapists who are open to this phenomenon could provide an anchor or sanctuary for the spirit personality's period of adjustment. Walk-ins in this situation do not have multiple personalities regardless of their background. Any sensitive therapist will be able to discern this. They will simply find too many sound, balanced aspects to the personality that do not equate as a disorder. Neurotic, yes, but then your whole world's mental posture is neurotic. It can't help it due to the levels of distortion that you define as the norm.

There is also a high probability that these walk-ins will be particularly skilled in dissociative states. Such states are valuable for accessing expanded levels of consciousness. Your psychiatric establishment defines these as dissociative "disorders." The capacity to attain these altered states is no indication of faulty mental health. However, when judged, they might be pushed into disorder.

One saving grace for walk-ins, zoo animals and everyone else, for that matter, is dreamtime. During your sleep you are free to leave your body and create balancing experiences to support your waking life. Many ET walk-ins go "home" at night for replenishment and support. Earth life is not easy.

A walk-in can put his/her waking consciousness behind this activity by suggesting before sleep a dream experience that will diffuse rage. On the waking plane, finding an acceptable expression for the rage is important, too. Rage is an impulse to action that is meant to move, not just sit there. Some sort of action is needed to give the energy a flow path. It is not likely for walk-ins to release this energy through aggressive, violent hostilities.

One path chosen for release can be physical disease. Anger often finds release through inflammatory symptoms and/or autoimmune diseases. These would include joint pain, throat infections and injuries to the body that are the expressions of frustration and rage directed against the self. However, the releasing of this energy through nonviolent alternatives does not have to be physical illnesses. As an energy release, any activity that moves aggressively will be very valuable: running, sports, expressive dancing, scrubbing a floor or climbing a mountain.

Sometimes the most difficult part of dealing with this problem is for the spirit to recognize that it is angry. Few walk-ins arrive fully conscious and totally aware of what arrival means. This would blow their neurological circuits, because the incoming spirit is from a level of consciousness that operates at a vibrational rate different from that on Earth. It would be something like your alternating and direct current; they are incompatible and cannot operate through the same wiring.

In terms of the body, major rewiring must be done before the incoming spirit can operate effectively through it. The adjustment is made on both sides. The neurological system of the body is altered and the spirit energy alters its vibrational rate to fit into the body more comfortably. This takes time. Therefore during the period of adjustment the incoming spirit needs to be aware that there is a just cause for the sense of rage that seems to be sourceless.

The pain of feeling caged and enraged can be made even worse if the walk-in allows guilt to compound the issue. Don't judge yourself; you have taken on something very difficult. Self-love and asking for help are necessary. We are working with counselors on your world to prepare them to accept and understand the kind of support that spirit replacements need.

Grieving the Loss of Self

Human consciousness on Earth is like a family of individuals residing under one name. The individuals represent the elements of consciousness that can be perceived in totality only by the higher self. They include the physical, mental, emotional and etheric bodies of consciousness as well as the multilevels of the unconscious.

The energy that animates this "family" is the spirit. When there is an exchange of spirits in the body, each family member will feel the loss of the departing spirit in his/her own way. The grief issue is based entirely on the perceptions and beliefs of the illusion-bound consciousness in dense physical life. This is the only level on which death and loss have any reality.

Walk-in adjustment includes balancing the new spirit and the bodies of consciousness that are reacting instinctively to the loss of the animating force they had recognized as their personal spirit. Bizarre as it might seem, there can be physical reactions similar to those that occur at the time of activation of the "death microbes" that break down the physical elements to be reabsorbed by the Earth. The body is saying that the energy it recognized as its personal life force is gone; therefore it must prepare to break down its elements to return to the soil.

Some of the illnesses walk-ins take on can be attributed to this sensing, though it is hard at this juncture of the Earth's evolution to determine the exact source of many of the complaints they are experiencing. The transition from dense matter to lightbodies creates the need to break down toxic matter from all the bodies of consciousness. When released through the physical body, it can produce the same complaints as the faulty death belief of the body.

Specific symptoms associated with grief include anything that approximates crying as part of the mourning pattern. This would include colds, allergies, eye infections, flu and similar release mechanisms.

As to the loss of the animating energy, the new spirit energy must reassure the bodies of consciousness that they are still supported by spirit. In the simplest terms this means that when you get sick and take appropriate actions to heal the physical body, remember to include your emotional, mental and astral bodies in your loving self-care.

The emotional body reacts in the strongest way to the loss of the original spirit. There is a definite sense of grief; some walk-ins have a vague, nagging sense of something missing, whereas others have a sense of catastrophe and deep mourning. This pain is often compounded by the doubts the self has about its perceptions of reality. Caught in the middle of the spirit exchange, the living-plane consciousness can feel confused, making the situation even more difficult.

To make it worse, this very real grief has no support from the walk-in's community, as would occur at the physical death of a family member. These elements can stunt the natural expression and release of mourning. The best advice we can offer is, if it feels like grief, it *is* grief. Honor it.

The natural mourning process is short-circuited because there is seldom an outer event such as a death in the family. It is a transformational process even if it is a clear-cut walk-in exchange. In this process there can be a repeated accumulation of feelings of loss, creating repeated episodes of grief.

From our perception, the concepts of braiding, blending and walking in do not begin to explain the intricacies of interweaving spirit and consciousness. For many walk-ins there has been some sort of gradual exchange: a prior period of communication, alternating occupation of the body or blending in some way. This is the process to which we are referring that occurs before a walk-in has a firm sense of his/her identity as a distinctly different spirit energy.

Many walk-ins and lightworkers have come to terms with the ideas about the transformation process under way on your world. They accept that the process involves clearing debris or purging toxins as the light energy comes in. The light moves in and the dark must move out. This translates as the physical symptoms involved in the elimination of toxins. The symptoms connected with this process most of you call being sick. You have been documenting for quite a while now that the mental and emotional bodies of consciousness go through similar purging processes. You all have experienced the painful aspects of these types of clearing.

Financial Breakdown

As old patterns are being shattered to make way for the age of light, all aspects and extensions of your lives are similarly affected. Ordinarily you have no problem equating health and wealth. Yet you don't see that going broke is just another form of purging and breaking patterns. You are dumping old finances to make way for new energy paths to open that bring in abundance.

Is there any real difference between going broke and a physical or emotional breakdown? It is just another way to throw out old stuff. If you view all as energy vibrations, you could actually find a way to feel good about hitting financial bottom. It is simply another step in getting rid of anything that holds back your progress. There is no reason to believe that when you are free of the old financial patterns, new means of financial support won't come through. They will come through and your new sources will be more in line with who you are now.

We feel that you can grasp this very easily. The real difficulty is fear. Your world's value system requires a dependable work force to sustain it. If you can't pull your share of the load, you are expendable. The lives you have taken over as walk-ins were deeply indoctrinated with these beliefs: Money means you can survive; without money your survival is questionable. That is very frightening. Humans feel fear when their lives are threatened.

The challenge to you, and it is a big one, is to trust that clearing out old financial patterns is part of your transformation into a lightbeing. And trust that you are guided, that you have valuable work to do and that you will be supported. From our position of expanded perception, we assure you that this is true.

There are many "folks back home" working with you on this project. Guides are always available; you are never alone. You don't even have to call out — just trust. We are aware, for this information is being transmitted by a guide from home.

FIVE

Cross-Gender Spirit Replacement

The Pleiadian Light

Our perception is that cross-gender walking-in is not very common, but in some cases it is useful. When the characteristics of the walk-out are already well-integrated, the stepping in of a spirit that resonates the energy of the opposite gender is a natural progression in development. This has the effect of fulfilling a project that has been considered by the original occupant as his/her path of growth and expansion.

One example is a female vehicle and life experience that was exploring victimhood, repression and powerlessness. She could have spent her life struggling and then gaining strength, self-reliance, feelings of worth and equality to an admirable degree. A walk-in spirit that resonates masculine energy could take over the challenge and give a greater resolution of balance and integration, thereby securing the same goal. This energy could bring in strength and a natural belief in the ability to actively participate in the Earth social structure from a point of recognized power. This person would seem to have suddenly gained a wonderful new strength.

The opposite circumstance could assist a masculine life to reach a greater level of richness in intuitive perceptions. These could have been be lacking, creating a void that the original occupant found limiting in his path of growth and expansion.

Suddenly, with a feminine spirit replacement, this man could be sensitive to his relationships in a new way and open to a more rapid expansion of consciousness due to a balancing and activation of right-brain activity. These are simplistic examples, but they give an idea of how cross-gender spirit replacement can establish a balance that will serve the walk-in and support the agenda for his/her mileage on the life path.

The perspective presented here is from the view of polarity — a given in this world consciousness. A broader view would reveal that all walk-in spirit energies are from more integrated levels than Earth. Walk-ins would not be impelled to take on the challenges of this world if they did not bring a more expanded perspective to assist in the transformation.

Let us reiterate that walk-ins are not superior beings. They are equal spirit energies who simply have a perspective that allows them to be of service in the Earth's transformation. Some extraterrestrial walk-ins come from worlds that still resonate polarized gender characteristics, but the dichotomy is nothing like the gender gulf on Earth. They are nevertheless able to resonate a balancing polar energy here.

Interdimensional energy usually comes from levels of total integration that have evolved beyond the reincarnational carousel, no longer representing physical expression. Except for angelic energy that has chosen to forego the physical experience entirely, the integrated light energies who are walking in to assist this world are the resolution level of otherworld cultures. They resonate certain overall qualities of the culture from which they ascended. Some of these qualities fall into definitions that veer toward the idea of the feminine or the masculine. For example, the Orion experience resonates masculinity even at its integrated level, whereas the Pleiadian light resonates a feminine quality.

From their place on their living plane, walk-ins can dialog with their spirit aspect on its integrated level. This would be like the receptionist or the doorman channeling, from its integrated position, the walk-in spirit that has taken over the life. If the integrated level is willing to give a name by which to identify itself for your convenience, you can then ascertain if there is a leaning toward one gender polarity or the other.

In the case of cross-gender replacements, the challenge of working out the gender conflicts will require an additional period of adjustment. The nature and the intensity of this challenge varies from one situation to another.

Remember, incoming concepts must be translated into the Earth value system to be understood by the caretaker. You might feel that there are people you don't like, then you judge yourself for being so critical. This might simply be your intuiting that certain people are not aligned with your agenda. They have agendas of equal value to themselves and the world evolution; they are just not the same as yours.

The Earth value system still operates on the illusion that if someone is right, then someone who thinks or acts differently must be wrong. This is one of the most difficult concepts to grasp in integrative metaphysics. There is really no yes or no; there is only yes and yes.

The cross-gender spirit replacements who are going through adjustment might translate their conflicts into fears about proper behavior or projects to undertake. Or the period of adjustment might play out as confusions in sexual preference that were not present before.

For the walk-in caught in this conflict we can say that as long as you operate from a base of self-love, you cannot do or be anything that is not aligned with your growth, your spiritual expansion or your reason for coming to assist this world. Self-love is the first and most important step on the spiritual path. It supports all your relationships and activities with love. Unconditional love is built on self-love. If it isn't, the result is like a stone structure built on water.

We remind all of you, whatever the challenges during your period of adjustment, spiritual guidance and angelic help are always available. In addition, more and more therapists and counselors are becoming open to the concepts of the age of light and can provide a sanctuary of understanding for your growth.

SIX

What Kind of Car Do You Drive?

The Pleiadian Light

When a spirit replacement is given the use of an Earth body, the characteristics inherent in the vehicle remain as well as the experiences of the life. This is like purchasing a secondhand car. Having a car to get around in is wonderfully convenient and gives you freedom to explore and experience extended dimensions of reality. That is what your body is — a miraculous vehicle made available to assist you in your work. The vehicle is not you; it is not your true identity. Most walk-ins sense this instinctively. However, it is easy to get drawn into the world value system that equates your worth with what you look like or the nationality or race to which your body belongs.

In the view of the extraterrestrial groups who are on the next rung of the process of integration, your history of enmity based on genetics is very difficult to understand. Humankind has waged wars, committed atrocities and enslaved groups based on the bodies they live in. When viewed from the spirit level, on which all are equal, this makes no sense whatsoever.

We know that the perceptions of "us" and "them" are built into the game plan in order to challenge you and expand your dimensions. Now the time has come to throw off these illusions to prepare for the next step on your journey of growth. Your attitudes might change if you viewed it as though all the people who owned Fords on your block decided to go to war against all

Chevrolet owners. What is there to fight about?

You have gained benefits from living in your extremely variegated world. The wide range of experiences available makes this world a wonderful opportunity for spirits to acquire almost any sort of growth experience they need for total soul enrichment.

The physical characteristics of different races hold opportunities. You each chose your "car model" before you walked in for the very characteristics it offered because you knew it would best serve you in whatever you wished to gain from this life on Earth. Even walk-ins align themselves with a walk-in situation that best serves their agenda. Your body is a valuable means of participating in the life you have chosen. Through it you can express, experience, create, grow, love and die. It is in your care. We suggest that you be grateful for whatever body you are working through, and remember that it is just your vehicle, not your identity.

Those who wail, "Why wasn't I born tall, dark and handsome?" or "Why don't I have a perfect figure and long blond hair?" are not aware that they are already in the body they felt would be perfect for them when they were making choices from the spirit level. Each of you knows on the level of your higher self what your agenda is on Earth. The vehicle you are working through is the one you felt would serve you best.

We will acknowledge that your world has some aspects that most otherworld cultures do not. Your DNA pool was seeded by several different extraterrestrial groups. On deep unconscious levels there are patterns of competition as to whose genetics would dominate your world. But even with this knowledge, the time has come to recognize your true spirit nature. As spirit, you are all equal.

We are belaboring this subject because we will be giving more information from time to time on the DNA patterning of this world. Many of the changes in the Earth's transformation into a world of light will involve alterations in the DNA of the species living on Earth. So we want it clearly understood that the changes in the vehicles through which you operate — the new skills on many levels — do not make you better than someone who has not yet brought in the new qualities. We don't want to start new wars. You are *all* perfect spirits.

SEVEN

Shining a New Light on the Dark Forces

Grace

All walk-ins come from levels that are more evolutionarily integrated than the Earth plane. Some are interdimensional energies in lightbodies that are not experiencing physical incarnations. Some are from extraterrestrial planetary cultures so integrated in polarity that the differences are not significant. When a walk-in from either situation encounters dark energies in Earth's polarized world, there is the possibility of underrating their reality and effect.

There is a wide range of aspects of Earth life that would fall on the dark side of a bell curve. When we begin to address their reality, there is the possibility of releasing from the dark corners of the ancient human psyche mythic demons and devils, black magic and evil practices whose power cannot be resisted. These are archaic beliefs and the result of a very good public relations campaign by the dark forces themselves. We wish to give you our assessment of the nature of these energies that will cast them into a more realistic light.

If you look at your history, you will remember that there was a time when microbes could not be seen ana were not understood. They were a parallel invisible world existing and interacting with you. Many misunderstandings and misconceptions abounded as to the causes of disease and other observable phenomena created by microbes.

When the first microscopes were invented, a light was shed on this hidden world. Exploration began which gave you a sense of understanding and the possibility of interacting with this world. Now you can control some of the negative effects of microbes and harness some of their positive characteristics.

There is another hidden world you are living with on a daily basis that affects you in ways you don't always realize. Understand that we never wish you to be fearful or feel at the mercy of these hidden energies. On the contrary, we are approaching this very carefully in order to support your own power in interacting with them — just as you retrieved your power over the microbes through science.

A world of energetic vibrations swirls around you all the time. These energies are perceived by only a small percentage of people on your plane. Because you still live in a polarized world, these energies affect your lives in both positive and negative ways. Generally speaking, the positive energies give support, nurture and love and the negative energies take your strength, worth, health and more. Walk-ins carry the ability to generate both types of energies.

As more light energy suffuses the world in this new age, it creates a greater sensitivity to, and more awareness of, the negative forces. Correspondingly, the dark forces, sensing a threat to their continued power in this world, are stepping up their activities. Therefore walk-ins in particular might have a period in which you are feeling attacked by these energies that recognize you as one whose primary purpose is to support the transition to integrated light energy.

We would like to give you some assistance, for you are never at the mercy of negative energy. Remember the microbial world that you now recognize and have some influence on. We will tell you that the hidden energy world is not so different from the world of germs.

You already know that you protect yourself from many diseases by simply establishing rituals of cleanliness. Bathing and maintaining a clean, germ-free environment reduces the possibility of attack. In addition, when you do get sick, you have all your healing endeavors to rebalance the situation.

The same opportunities are available to deal with the attack of negative energies, but here you will be generating light energies to clear the dark ones from your personal energy sphere, no matter what their source. The true power to banish negative energy comes from you.

We would like to give you a meditation you can use as a personal-hygiene ritual — the same as brushing your teeth or washing your face.

While standing, visualize a brilliant beam of white light coming in through the top of your head and suffusing your whole body. See the light radiating out from you in all directions. Then see the light flowing down from your feet into the ground, deep into the center of the Earth. See the light securely tethered to the Earth's core and the nurturing energy of the Earth traveling back up the flow of light to support you.

Next, visualize the brilliant white light flowing down your arms and out your hands. Slowly turn in a clockwise circle, directing the energy beams from your hands outward to sever any negative attachments in time, space and all dimensions. Demand that the dark energies leave your energy sphere and go into the light. Speak this aloud with vehemence if you are in a position to do so. You are not launching an attack. You are demanding the sovereignty of your position from a point of active power. Direct the energies to go in peace, but they must go! You can call guides or angelic help to lead the dark energies into the light. You are simply integrating them with their true source, for all is light. In a sense, the gift of light is your best defense.

As a final step, visualize yourself pulling in swirls of blue and green light to fill your energy sphere. Then scatter sparkling diamonds of white light in the swirls of blue and green. Finish by seeing your energy sphere expanding out to infinity.

We recommend this meditation as part of your regular routine. You would not consider that just because you took a bath last month you are permanently free of germs growing on your body. You will find in this routine another tool to assist you during your period of adjustment to this world.

In the long run you will free yourself from any effects of the dark energies by your progress on this plane. As you bring in more light energy, you will move onto levels of reality that are simply beyond the perceptions of the negative energies. If they can't see you, they don't feel threatened and they won't attack. It is as simple as that.

EIGHT

The Walk-in/Animal Connection

The Pleiadian Light

The walk-in connection with the animal world is more a closer interaction than a sympathetic resonance with all God's creatures. The majority of walk-in consciousness is from otherworld cultures or interdimensional levels. The type of communication used by most otherworld entities who are "ahead" of you on the evolutionary path is closer to the way animals communicate with each other on this plane.

An intuitive understanding is obtained by direct access. Intuitive understanding is actually a contradiction in terms, so we prefer to substitute the word "accommodation." Animals communicate by directly accommodating the total message, without the linear progression of a concept given a verbal vehicle. Animal accommodation uses many elements considered extrasensory by humans. Many of your pets, however, go to great lengths to operate within your mode of communication.

Language is a clever creation, a product of intellectual expansion and exploration believed by humans to represent superior intelligence. But it is a communication that substitutes symbols for concepts. Language can hamper extrasensory data that come through in feelings that are difficult or impossible to translate. Language is a game that has been created to bridge the gulf between individuals caused by polarity and separation, both the archetypal separation from God and the separation between individual humans.

Earth animals exist in a polarized world too, but still retain a sense of unity with their species and with all nature. This enables them to communicate at high levels of telepathy. However, they also have empathy, extended perceptions that include energy fields (auric vision), a keen attunement to fluctuations in the natural world and an absence of ego interference. Because of this range of communication skills — a polar opposite to intellectual language — the animals hold a superior position.

Put this into one of your TV scenarios: Some "poor little alien" agrees to take over an Earth life. He comes in with enthusiasm and great expectations. Then he finds himself in the midst of a chaotic Earth life and quickly realizes that those who communicate in the manner he accommodates best are animals. In addition, the communication with animals has much greater clarity and truth than he finds in human exchanges.

The Earth is a theater world. Everyone is playing parts, writing parts, creating dramas. This is the Earth game and it is the only game in town. Therefore, you poor little aliens have to find a way to accommodate it. We are not in any way putting it down; we are just having some fun playing the game, too. It is a world of delightful illusion with golden sequins and bright lights. Bravo!

Most extraterrestrial civilizations you are currently aligned with do not play this game. However, the Pleiadians still feel "the play's the thing." Most of the Pleiadian contact with you at this time is from their fourth-dimensional level of development, which is your next level. Even though their communication is telepathic, they also have a verbal language that enhances telepathy. Their theater presentations are still valuable to them for the vicarious expansions they stimulate and for the pure joy of the experience. (Incidentally, a high percentage of the muses who inspire Earth artistic creations are Pleiadian artists working intuitively with Earth counterparts.) But even Pleiadians feel more comfortable with animals than with many humans.

As for other ET cultures and interdimensional entities, animals respond to them easily, lovingly and with gratitude for their superior skills. If you are a lightworker on Earth, no matter how you arrived or where you came from, you might find that some of your closest friends are animals. Don't let anyone convince you that this is neurotic behavior indicating an inability to relate to people. Your animal friends might really be the creatures closest to your understanding and perception of reality.

Another aspect we wish to address and confirm is that there are both animal spirits and animal walk-ins. Some animal spirits who have great wisdom and know well the natural world of Earth will project their consciousness into the pet of a lightworker, forming a working partnership with the human. (In this partnership are elements of the concept of the "familiar," in which the human taps the animal's perceptions.)

This contributes an integrated stream of data that assists the lightworker's intuitive perceptions. More important, there is a balancing in which the animal takes on some of the channeling of energy in the living experience. So rather than yelling at your cat for throwing up on the rug, you might thank her for purging some aspect of your living situation that you "can't stomach."

Your pets are working in an equal partnership. Watch them. Listen to them. The care, the learning and the growth go both ways.

PART 2

TRANSFORMATIONAL GUIDELINES for LIGHTWORKERS and WALK-INS

NINE

As If It Weren't Hard Enough

Hannah Beaconsfield

Trials of Transition

As if it were not hard enough for walk-ins to take over alien lives and heal sick bodies and minds, they must do so while dramatic transformations are going on in those bodies, minds and the world around them. This time in our history is definitely not business as usual. There is a momentous change affecting the Earth and the bodies of all who inhabit the planet. There is a dramatic alteration in the vibratory rate of this world.

The physical nature of Earth has progressed from an etheric mass of gases to a dense world of flesh and trees, rocks and steel. Density has reached its maximum development and is at the end of its downward trajectory, which has defined the progress of physical reality. This trajectory has taken world consciousness to the maximum degree of separation from its spiritual source. The return path will gain momentum as it is drawn back toward the Source, or the beginning.

In the case of a planetary evolution and the spirit energy that supports it, the return trajectory represents a reintegration with All That Is, or God. It also entails a return from very dense physical structuring to a progressively lighter physical reality in terms of wavelengths of vibration that differentiate darkness from light. The light is also the God source of all worlds and universes expanding to infinity.

There are many physical symptoms connected with this process of transformation. If you talk to others who are exploring similar paths, you will hear a litany of symptoms that are being experienced by many people. I've come to refer to these discomforts as transformational dementia and transitional flu. Some of the many physical complaints include mental fogginess, memory problems, chronic low-grade infections, episodes of toxic purging with nausea and diarrhea, headaches, upper-respiratory congestion, allergies, weight gain, visual and auditory phenomena and more.

A quick sketch of the process affecting the Earth and each individual on Earth is as follows: As the energy and vibration of light moves onto this plane, all physical life is altered by it. As human bodies take in the light energy there is a natural purging of dark or negative energies from all bodies of consciousness. This includes toxins from the physical body as well as negative emotions from the emotional body of consciousness. The mental body also purges old belief patterns that no longer serve. The vibrations of light are taken into the astral body first and then progress to the "descending" bodies of consciousness in the clearing process.

The entry of light into the body also activates a latent potential in the Earth DNA that releases additional strands of genetic coding. These strands hold the coding for the transmutation of the species. You might say this is a light-activated mutation process. The new DNA characteristics represent the next dimensional levels for Earth planetary life — the ascension of this world.

There is always a clearing of debris to make way for the new. This process is causing the plethora of symptoms and complaints that so many are experiencing now. The whole planet could not handle this simultaneously, for it would be in total chaos. So at the head of the pack are the ones who are gaining an understanding of the process to help those who follow.

[One source of comfort for the trials of transition is a booklet called "I'm O.K., I'm Just Mutating." See Directory.]

Mutation Management: Addressing Transformational Complaints

The great mental fog. The primary complaint is short- (and not-so-short-) term memory loss, when you aren't nearly old enough to have Alzheimer's disease. Or else you're old enough to have Alzheimer's and you are worried that you *do*. Ruling out Alzheimer's and any other similar condition, this disturbance in a normally acute mind is due (according to my channeled sources) to a form of rerouting of neurological pathways as the two hemispheres of the brain begin to operate in a more integrated manner. In other words, not only can't you remember where you left your watch, but your brain can't remember the pathways the neurons must follow to remember the watch.

Trust your brain. It has evolved and made incredible adjustments through millennia. The ability to accurately remember will return, but when it does it will be operating in a new way. Instead of being like a file cabinet, which you utilize in a linear manner ("Let's see, I remember I had my watch in my hand when I was timing how long it takes a squirrel to bury a nut; then I went into the kitchen . . ."), the new brain wiring will work more like a computer ("Where did I leave my watch? Please access"). The answer will pop onto the screen of your mind. At first it will take a while between the access command and the answer, but gradually the computing time will get shorter and shorter until it is an instantaneous process that you will no longer even be aware of.

One other point connected to the rewiring process is weight gain. Some of the extra weight is water retained for increased electrical conductivity. Also, the weight gain acts as a shock absorber because the new levels of electromagnetic energy are something of a jolt compared with what the body has been used to.

Marshmallow time. Feeling that time is running slower or faster than usual is part of the light-activated changes. Often there is a sense of being stuck in time despite the continued linear flow registered by the clock. This is due to the alteration of the physical vehicle and the passenger consciousness moving out of alignment with the linear time structure. The linear time structure is a cornerstone of dense physical reality. When we begin to pull out of its framework, we cannot expect to utilize time in the same way we once did.

Einstein gave us the information that time stands still at the speed of light. That is what we are moving toward — light speed — but not tomorrow and not in the lifetime of anyone alive now. The path we are on is the path to the source of all light. As we step onto that path we are already altering our relationship to time, and we feel it.

The DNA flip. This is the idea of the release of additional strands of DNA — which I found confusing. I asked for channeled information on how this would happen. Where would the strands come from?

The explanation I was given is that the additional strands won't unfold within the present double-helix pattern. The expansion of the DNA is really a flip into a parallel or probable body pattern that already has the additional strands.

There are also variations in the number of strands in the new bodies, which range from three to twelve, maybe more. Not everyone will move to the same number of strands when they flip. Individuals will move to the level of change that they can handle, depending on their level of development. There can be a progression of flips to reach a desired level.

The important point here is that the flip actually occurs on the astral level. The astral body moves into an alternate astral body that already contains additional DNA strands; then the new DNA characteristics begin to move gradually through the successive bodies of consciousness until they reach the densest, or physical, level, making changes as they go. This is still a temporal world where time is the vehicle of change.

Allergies. When I was a kid hardly anyone had allergies. Now almost everyone is allergic to something. About five or six years ago I had so many allergies, I was close to being what is called a universal reactor. When I asked for channeled information on the allergy situation, I was given an explanation which, though highly unscientific, was very helpful to me.

The Pleiadian Light explained that when our bodies are very

dense they are able to handle, absorb, store and even use a wide range of toxins. When we move into lightbodies, the new vibrational rate allows toxins to simply pass through the body, causing no harm. However, the time of transformation between those two points, which is different for each individual, is a time of chaos for the immune system. Toxins enter the body but can't pass through or be absorbed and defused. The body marks them as invaders that must be fought. So a complex alarm system goes off, causing all sorts of reactions. The immune system can get confused by the changes in toxin recognition, and when it loses the ability to recognize "self," autoimmune diseases occur.

The Pleiadian Light assured me that as we progress through this transformation we will move beyond these allergic reactions. I am pleased that I can attest to that. After five years of intense allergies, I am almost free of reactions. I still have some mild pollen problems and a couple of food reactions, but compared with what I used to experience, I feel cured.

Reactivated energy sites. The human body has evolved the process of aging and death in a much shorter time than the original life span on this world. Short life spans allow a rapid turnover of reincarnational experiences. Painful life experiences that promoted rapid learning and spiritual progress were chosen by many as this world moved into its deepest density.

As much as I hate to admit it, painful experiences often gain a level of progress for us that can't be attained as rapidly any other way. These are personal choices, but I must put a word in for kindness and self-love. The time of pain-forced transformation is coming to an end. The future rests on the care and value of the self.

During the evolution toward short life spans, certain glandular centers in the body were programmed to shut down or atrophy shortly after adulthood. Three such glandular centers are the thymus, the pineal gland and the limbic system in the brain.

These centers support longevity. When reactivated, they support revitalization and rejuvenation of the body. The thymus is a primary center of the immune system. The pineal gland supports cerebral chemical activity, allowing for expanded perceptions of the reality spectrum. The limbic system supports the integration of various systems of the bodies of consciousness.

The light vibrations coming into the body are reactivating these centers, altering the code that signals them to shut down. For those who are experiencing reactivation, there is a spectrum of symptoms connected with the process.

Symptoms of Brain-Center Reactivation

The thymus center is located midway between the base of the throat and the heart. As it is reactivated there is often a congestion and release through the lungs and bronchi. This can take the form of colds and flu.

Activity in the limbic and pineal areas can be the source of headaches at the base of the skull. Pressure from the reactivation of this area can cause ear problems such as inner ear pressure and ringing sounds. In the eyes it can cause various visual symptoms from the increase of vitreous floaters to flashing lights on the visual periphery.

Many symptoms of transformational changes can have assorted causes, so I recommend you approach health care in a holistic way. Conventional medical science is the result of tremendous accomplishments in this world's technological growth and has a valuable place in treating the body, but the revival of ancient healing methods and the creation of new inventive modalities are equally valid. The most important skill in healing is the individual's ability to hear what his/her body is saying and giving it the best care available.

Many symptoms of physical transformation can be eased by allowing all the bodies of consciousness opportunities to express the energies that need to be released and then supporting the integrative process. Activities like sports, dancing, drumming and singing do both. All the fun things we've been taught to consider frivolous are the very activities that can assist our transformation into bodies of light.

TEN

Chakra Energy Centers

The Seven Major Centers

Grace

The chakras, the energy centers of the body, link the bodies of consciousness: astral, mental, emotional and physical. There are many chakra points in the body; however, we will consider only the major centers that are located along the spinal column. It is through these centers that the energetic influences flow between the physical vehicle and the energy sphere or aura that surrounds it. This is an energy system similar to the circulatory and nervous systems that carries the energy throughout the physical body. Oriental medicine understands this system and has charted the meridians, which are used in acupuncture. Traditionally, there have been seven major centers along the spinal column.

Root chakra. The first center is at the base of the spine, or coccyx, associated with the color red. This chakra is connected with survival in this world and your relationship with the Earth as your physical source. It is associated with instinctive impulses and the fears that support survival by the fight-or-flight impulse.

Wellspring chakra. It generates and stores energy and resonates the color orange. It is the center for sexuality and procreation, but also emanates the energy that creates civilizations, works of art or ideas. Generically, it supports all creativity.

Solar plexus chakra. The color yellow is its signature. It is the center linked to the emotional body of consciousness. It holds the energies for the emotions that support and are generated by life on Earth. These are emotions that fall into polarized categories of positive and negative.

Heart chakra. It is connected with the color green and is the center of unconditional love — the spiritual love that encompasses all. It is the center for the love of God to flow through us onto this plane.

Throat chakra. Represented by the color blue, this center is closely connected to your personal expression in this world, whether through your profession, relationships or the expression of yourself as an individual in your society.

Brow chakra, or third eye. Deep midnight blue or indigo is its color. This energy center is most closely connected to extrasensory perceptions or the ability to sense intuitively and perceive beyond what is known through the use of normal faculties.

Crown chakra. Violet is the resonant color of the center for enlightenment, the expansion of consciousness and a direct connection to the source of all energy, or God.

Two New Major Chakras

Grace

There are chakras that extend above and below the body, linking you with your society, planet, solar system, galaxy and so forth on through infinity. In addition to the seven major chakras, there are two more that are emerging at this time in your development, assuming major positions in the spinal lineup.

Thymus chakra. This center is located halfway between the heart and throat centers. On your plane the color turquoise most closely approximates its vibrations. This center is linked to the thymus gland and the immune system.

Skull-base chakra. Located where the spinal column meets the skull, it blends the red of the root chakra with the dark blue and violet of the other cranial centers to resonate a color like magenta or maroon. This center forms a triangle with the other two head centers and makes all three very sensitive to sonic stimulation. It is connected to the limbic center of the brain.

There is another aspect of the chakra system that must be

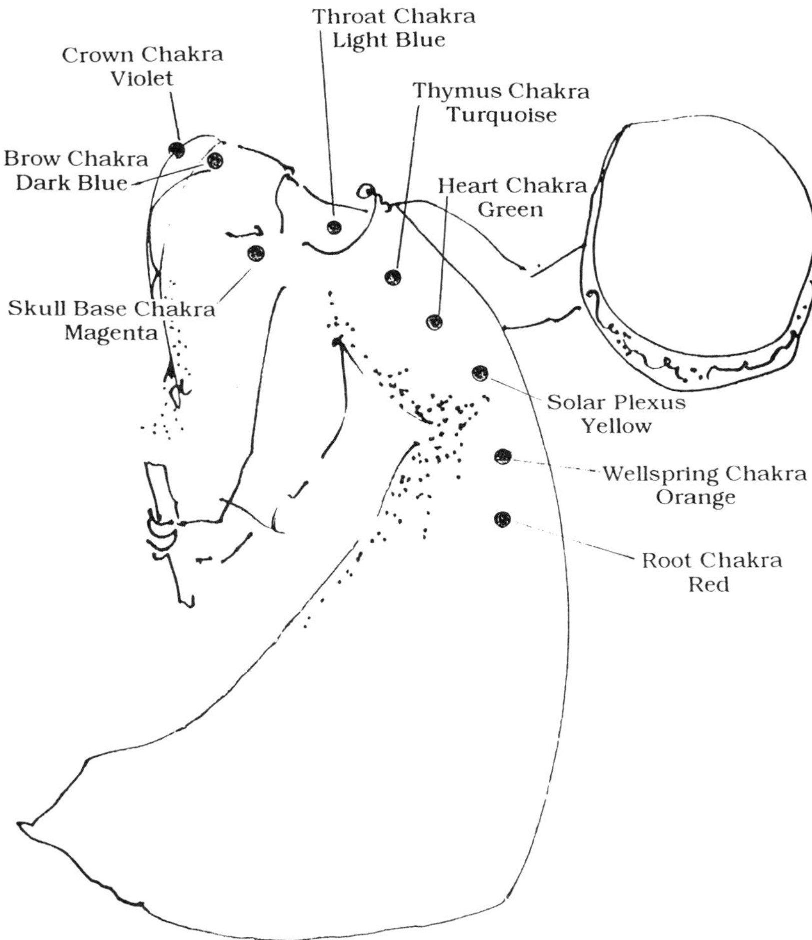

The Chakras or Energy Centers

addressed. These centers operate to one degree or another in the natural process of living. However, when you begin to consciously work to open and activate these energy centers, a clearing process begins. The reactions might be different for each chakra and individual, but they can include a purging of blocking energies. This takes the form of releasing negative emotions and clearing the physical body through symptoms you consider illness. In ancient texts this is referred to as the rising of the kundalini energy that opens, clears and activates the chakra system.

A great deal of esoteric material has been written about the chakra system in metaphysical texts. This limited introduction above is included for those who are unfamiliar with this system.

The Once and Future Chakras

The Pleiadian Light

As the vibrational changes of the age of light move onto your plane, the two chakras experiencing activation — the thymus and skull-base chakras — are joining the seven major chakras.

The thymus and skull-base energy centers were active in your ancient past. They originated from the DNA that was bred into the Earth animal forms by the extraterrestrial colonists who first established bases here. These energy centers closed down in the majority of your humanoid vehicles as you moved into a denser material world.

This was part of your evolutionary process in a world consciousness that was exploring the polarization of all its elements. This process went to its limits in density and darkness and now the pendulum is swinging back to the light.

Both the thymus and skull-base energy centers are connected to aspects of intuitive communication — the thymus aligning with planetary life energy and the skull base aligning with universal life energy. The thymus chakra is a center whose energies link you in a more expanded way to your physical life plane — your planet and all living elements on it, known and unknown. As you begin on your path into the light, this chakra is now reawakening and you will be experiencing many new perceptions, feelings and skills.

The new perceptions will include how you perceive the planet on which you live. Attitudes will change toward animals, plants and the energy consciousness of Earth. (This is already happening.) The activation will also connect you with elements that will enable you to harness creative and manifesting energies in ways you currently believe impossible or miraculous.

You will be able to perceive characteristics of matter beyond those you presently understand. You will find that molecular structures can be disassembled and reassembled, enabling you to transform matter. Structural alteration will include regenerating and rejuvenating the physical body, for the thymus center is the site of the internal fountain of youth. Other new skills will include the creation of solid substances from thin air by thoughts that magnetize elements to converge into the desired form.

Technology will evolve to support and develop these new skills. The first step will be the opening of the thymus, or "high heart" chakra. This will link your energy in an intimate way with all the elements and aspects of your natural world. The adjoining chakras contribute to the process, too. To give you some idea of the mechanism involved here, you might say that the powerful energy of unconditional love (via heart chakra) is charged with energy from the thymus center and given active expression (via throat chakra) in the world.

When this chakra was previously active, humans lived close to nature, instinctively understanding the natural laws. The closing down of this center was part of the challenge you took on when you agreed to explore dense physical reality and separation from Source. It was like saying to your collective self, "How clever and creative can I be at surviving if I voluntarily remove one of my most important senses?" Well, you were clever enough to evolve a complex technology working primarily through your intellect. This is like saying you did it with only half a brain.

However, this game is losing its challenge as you round the bend and move toward the light. This light takes the form of both enlightenment and a lightening of physical density. The change to less dense physical matter is already under way. This occurs on the astral (etheric) body of consciousness first, then filters through to the physical body. The change involves throwing off negative-energy toxins from all the bodies of consciousness. On the physical level you might experience many symptoms you will regard as disease or dysfunction.

The thymus center will assist you during these changes because it activates your immune system, clears toxins and balances your total hormonal picture. Some of your degenerative diseases involving hormonal imbalances are partially due to the decline in endocrine activity that the body has programmed in this area. Well, that missing part is becoming active again.

If you include this center in your chakra meditations, it will become more active and fall into its rightful place in the chakra system. It is wide-ranging in its influence, much like the heart center. Perhaps that is why it is sometimes referred to it as the high heart.

The skull-base energy center is a window into your world for other dimensions of consciousness. For those on Earth, it acts as a receiver of information from other dimensions. This center is connected with channeling and other psychic arts. It is also a center for interworld, intergalactic communications. You might say it is the first touchdown site for ETs to open communication with your plane.

There will be a mass reawakening of these two chakras when your world moves into the age of light and is ready to take on a conscious ability to tap the universal data bank. This is conscious channeling, and it is the future for the Earth human species. These are truly doors to both an ancient and an entirely new way of living on your magnificent world.

The Cranial Triangle

The Pleiadian Light

We have an overview of the chaos of your world at the present time (1996). It shows a shattering of patterns — not just the habituated cultural patterns, but also the individual body patterns that are riding the two-strand DNA.

Light energy has a vibratory counterpart in sonic energy. This affects the human body and the world by shattering dense energy forms in much the same way that a tone can shatter glass. This is currently opening up space for the lightbodies (human and world) to expand. In the body there is an awakening of the brain sector that is stimulated by visible light. As this vibratory energy enters the body it is read as light energy, which affects the pineal gland, also light-responsive. This has been your dark age, despite your belief that technological achievement equals enlightenment.

There have also been limitations in the operations of the limbic portion of the brain. Some of the hormones have been available for only limited periods of the human life span, whereas others required a specific stimulus to activate them when others were dormant. These portions will also experience expanded function.

When the more refined vibratory light of spirit "hits" the body, it activates the skull-base energy center. There is then a linkup with the brow and crown chakras to create a triangle that, as a unit, potentiates the qualities of each. The apex of the triangle is the crown chakra. These chakras handle transcendental and extrasensory data. Generally speaking, the brow center (the third eye) handles perception of all that is beyond normal sight. The skull base is a communication center for the exchange of telepathic information. The crown is the center of transcendent enlightenment.

The cranial triangle, once energetically hooked up, is extremely sensitive to sound as a vibratory activator. Certain sounds are harmonious with the triangle, whose resonance brings the three cranial centers into perfect balance. (Some of these sounds are the sounds of nature.) In addition there are scents or aromas that work alone or with sounds to assist balance. Balance aligns perception, communication and enlightenment to support the expanded humanoid species that will inhabit the age of light.

ELEVEN

Tools of Assistance

Hands of Light

The Pleiadian Light

We wish to present material to assist you in the transmutation process as it affects your body. Understand that entering the age of light requires shifts in the energy fields of the Earth and all living things upon it. Changes in these energy fields will produce physiological changes in the human body.

As the bodies of consciousness take in more light energy, there is a continual shifting of balances. This repeated need for rebalancing can be supported by many of the holistic healing endeavors such as chiropractic, acupuncture, massage and energy balancing. In addition, gradually moving to a lighter diet and drinking more water is helpful, as is exercise.

You can also help yourself with this transition by channeling energy through your hands to your own body. Everyone has this ability to one degree or another, and with practice the ability will grow stronger. It is one of the skills that will be surfacing as you move into the expanded versions of yourselves.

It is presently understood in metaphysics that the right hand gives energy and the left receives it. As you move into the integration of polarities, you might find yourself impulsively using your less dominant hand more often. Left- or right-handedness will become less specialized. Both hands will have equal abilities to give and receive. The energy being channeled will then be generic and the effect of the energy on matter will depend on intent.

If you intuitively sense that it is right for you to continue to use your hands in the polarized manner for now, do so. If not, you can use both hands equally and state your intent as to how you wish the energy to serve you.

Repressed or denied emotions that have been stored as pockets of negative energy are often given expression and release through illness and pain. Channeling energy through your hands can release and ease such discomfort.

In the case of pockets of negative energy, you might direct the giving (active) energy to break open the pockets of blocked energy, then direct the receiving (magnetic) energy to draw out the dark emotions. Visualize a white light around your hands that transmutes this energy and releases it harmlessly into space. You can do this exercise in a meditation over each of your chakras or over a part of the body that is expressing pain.

Gemstones used as tools can enhance and further define the energy channeled through the hands. Clear quartz, for example, acts as a potentiator and can be programmed to act as a filter for a particular intent.

Sonics can also assist your hands. We suggest humming a tone as you channel energy through your hands. We prefer humming rather than toning when you are working on yourself because the vibrations are held within the body and set up a resonance. If you are familiar with kinesiology testing, you could hum a scale and muscle-test for the strongest reaction. If you do not know how to use muscle-testing, you could hum a scale and sense which tone feels right, or you could intuitively allow a tone to find its place. Try two tones a fifth apart, sounding the higher note first, then the lower one for its centering and balancing effect.

Self-Balancing with Sonics

Grace

We wish to present some ideas and techniques to assist you in balancing your bodies of consciousness. We will move away from the word "healing" and replace it with "balancing." *Healing* implies that there is something injured or wrong. As long as you hold the concept of healing, you inevitably create its polar opposite, disease, for healing cannot exist without disease.

When you use the idea of balancing instead of healing, you don't inflict on yourself any negative feelings that can cause guilt and fuel self-hatred. We wish to promote your loving acceptance of yourself.

The technique we are presenting is a means by which you can alter the electromagnetic and chemical activity of the brain. This technique can also be used to open and activate the chakras in the head as well as the glands connected to these energy centers.

The technique is as follows:

Place yourself in a deep state of relaxation by way of meditation or trance induction. Visualize brilliant white light entering your crown chakra, aligning all of your energy centers and exiting through the root chakra. See the light descend deep into the center of the Earth, securely grounding you and allowing the Earth's energy to rise up and support you.

Direct this white light to flow down your arms and out your hands. At this point the light energy is generic. You can direct it to have a specific effect by a simple request. In this case you will request that the energy support the balancing of feelings and moods. The examples we will address at this time are the moods of fearfulness, anxiety and depression.

Place your palms over your ears tightly to dampen any external sounds. Now, if you are feeling down and want to lift your mood, hum two notes a fifth apart, like C to G. Keep your hands at your ears. Hum the C first, then slide up to G and hold it as long as possible. Be sure to hum it, for that will quickly set up a powerful resonance in your head. If you are feeling anxious or agitated, you can reverse the notes. Hum the G first, then slide down to C and hold that.

Repeat this several times. Each individual must sense how many repetitions is personally effective. Sometimes practicing this technique several times a day in short periods is more valuable.

Whenever we present these various ideas for directing and manipulating energy for yourselves, our intention is to provide directions to a path you can explore. Those who are excited by such ideas can take these directions and map out expanded applications. In this case we suggest that hand-channeled energy can be combined with sound vibrations, and that musical intervals can form useful vibratory effects.

These tones and frequencies have correlations in colors, gemstones, animal energies and so forth. They are available for you to explore. Tapping into and applying this energy is part of the leap in consciousness connected to the age of light. Harnessing the multilevels of consciousness is the next step in your evolution.

TWELVE

Super 3D: A Tool for Integrating the Brain-Mind Complex

The Pleiadian Light

Ever since I can remember I have had episodes in which my eyes would get locked in some strange sort of vision I called super 3D. I've done work as a film editor, and when I would concentrate on cutting images and making splices, I sometimes got stuck in this visual mode and had a really hard time getting out of it. I thought it must be some kind of an affliction, but I wasn't concerned enough to seek medical help.

A couple of years ago the fad of stereograms was very popular. I recognized that there was some kind of connection between this phenomenon and my locked-eye syndrome. I felt that by viewing stereograms one could somehow enhance psychic abilities like auric vision. I also thought it was a lot of fun, so I bought five or six books of those images and someone gave me large posters of them for my birthday.

Recently I was viewing some videotapes of a Flower of Life workshop given by Drunvalo Melchizedek. He was teaching techniques for viewing images in this manner. He stated that pictures intended to be viewed in this way have been found in ancient ruins around the world. He said that this was an ancient mystery-school method for teaching how to integrate the two hemispheres of the brain, and that while you are perceiving the 3D effect, both sides of the brain are operating simultaneously.

I was so excited about this information that I immediately asked my guides for some channeled information on the subject, which follows.

— Hannah Beaconsfield

We can say that there are very important cerebral processes going on when you practice stereogram viewing. This endeavor does assist the crossover and integration of the hemispheres of the brain. It is like a perceptual workout gym for the brain-mind complex, preparing you for the integrated future into which you are moving.

The modes of viewing practiced in most of the recently published books on the subject are either cross-eyed viewing or straight on, disengaged vision. These two different methods enhance different sets of skills.

The cross-eyed method is more closely connected with feminine viewing and is often easier for females. It serves to integrate the cerebral functioning in a way that enhances the inner intuitive aspects of expanded perceptions, including clairvoyance, clairaudience and prophecy.

The straight-on, disengaged viewing is more of a masculine-type cerebral integrative method. You will see doctors do this when they palpate a body area. It is like throwing their eyes out of focus and putting their consciousness into their hands as organs of sight. This method of integrated viewing enhances the perceiving of external intuitive phenomena, including auric vision, dowsing, sensing energy fields and determining magnetic polar directions, like an intuitive compass.

You can see how these two different methods have served the traditional needs of the male and female roles in your history up to now. The inner intuitive served the female in her caregiving, based on the intuitive perceiving of needs, the sensing of rightness, the reading of a person's state and holding the heart of the family unit. The masculine intuitive skills serve the one who goes out into the world, the one who needs expanded skills for survival in the world of hunting and protecting his family.

When you view many of the stereogram images in the popular books today, almost all the pictures can be viewed either cross-eyed or straight on. The image will often be concave when viewed cross-eyed and convex when viewed straight on. This aligns with the outward and inward modes of male/female polar viewing explained above.

If you find that viewing one way is easier for you, spend

more time practicing the alternate method to balance your individual integrative processes. A broad spectrum of physical and mental activities take place when you practice viewing stereograms, and concurrent multilevel changes occur while you hold the integrated state. It is a valuable tool you can explore to understand its implications. It is a power your humanoid species is just beginning to understand. The integrated brain-mind complex is much greater than the sum of its parts.

THIRTEEN

Forced Consciousness Expansion

The Pleiadian Light

The disturbingly high level of abuse and victimization on your world is part of the clearing of the dark and hidden elements of Earth life. These patterns are being exposed to the light so they can be understood and healed. If your world consciousness were not yet ready to heal this pattern, there would still be general denial and the victims would be blind to it to a degree.

Please try to understand the level from which we view your world. It is a removed overview. We are not insensitive to the individuals who are in unbearable pain. We understand there are many other aspects of abusive situations, for your reality is multidimensional. We wish to defuse some of the pain connected with feelings of guilt and talk about the confusion around why, if you create your own reality, such a life situation might be taken on.

We feel that if we give our overview we can help you see your way out of a deep, dark forest. When you are lost in the woods you can see only endless trees, dark shadows and doom. From our view, you can see that there are perimeters as well as a path to freedom.

Our view of a repeated life patterning of sexual abuse is that it can dam sexual energy in order to force open the upper energy centers (chakras) of the body in a rapid, powerful way. The trauma of adult rape has similar effects on consciousness.

Forced consciousness expansion is taken on at mass levels when a world culture feels it needs to make rapid spiritual growth. Many have undertaken this dangerous means of expanding to spirit levels because a major concerted effort is needed to push your world over the top of the mountain of change. It is the point of critical mass when you switch from darkness to begin the journey into light.

We say that this is dangerous because the adjustments inherent in kundalini opening and the reactions to being abused can create a life with an extremely painful inner terrain. The saving grace is that as consciousness expands, skills are brought in that help to handle such a difficult situation. There is a very delicate balance that has to be maintained so that the life can be sustained.

Walk-in situations are another level of disturbance and adjustment. Only extraordinary times would warrant this level of repeated trauma with the expectation that life would still be viable — and, what's more, influential.

Damming a powerful genetic energy force by trauma for the purpose of sustaining the species can be used as an alternate method to impel a major change in the species. The diverted energy supports the birth of a new species of humans. This makes perfect sense to the higher self when it chooses life circumstances that are intended to work within the mass consciousness of the species.

To the ego self and the caretaker consciousness in a walk-in situation, the pain of these chosen life situations seems unbearable. We do not present this information lightly or without consideration for the pain many have taken on. Rather, we are presenting this as gently as possible to help individuals release themselves from the overwhelming question about *why* they were so badly damaged. It is our intention to give a broader picture so that those who are damaged can allow themselves to consciously understand their contribution to the massive changes now taking place.

When you dam a river, the water backs up and spreads out, destroying plants and animal life. However, the power of the energy generated by the dam can also create electricity to light a city. If you had your home in such an area, your loss would not be lessened by the wider view, but you would no longer feel helpless against forces you could not understand. You would see your participation in a larger plan. If this eases the pain of the trauma even a fraction, it is worthwhile.

When the damming of sexual energy blocks the second chakra (wellspring energy center), the life energy forces open the higher centers, which align the physical body with expanded consciousness. This form of forced consciousness expansion requires a great deal of support from family, psychological counselors and groups of people who have had similar experiences and who can provide mutual support.

The rapid formation of social structures of support for sexual trauma victims in the last decade indicates that the mass consciousness is aware of the challenges that the abused have taken on. We too add our support by reminding all who are in pain that there are angelic and spirit guides who are always close by and respond to every call.

FOURTEEN

Reincarnational Depression

The Pleiadian Light

A serious depression can have emotional and/or genetic sources, but there is another source that's not always explored. Often the cause is carried on the astral template. Astral consciousness is the model after which the "descending" bodies of consciousness pattern themselves.

All changes, including growth and illness, as well as patterns carried from former lives are aspects that enter the total life experience from the astral body. These patterns are carried by a vibrational network similar to the way that DNA carries genetics.

The stuff of the astral body is light waves. The astral body acts like a prism for the light energy that is the life force of your spirit. That spirit energy is white light. As it passes through the prism of the astral body, it is separated into the spectrum of frequencies that activate the chakra centers and influence the various bodies of consciousness connected to the chakra centers. For example, a strand of green light that flows through the emotional body produces feelings of love. As it moves through the mental body it stirs thoughts about self-love, love of others and love of All That Is. At the point of its terminus in the body it affects the heart and lungs.

Scars from former life experiences are carried by the astral body. When the body is being formed as a fetus or when later in life that pattern is reactivated in response to a stimulus, this astral scar will be reflected in the body in one way or another. A simple example would be birthmarks. Often a blow or damage to a part of the body in one life will be carried as a birthmark in a later, related incarnation.

Major depression is most closely connected to a former life experience involving a prolonged period of extreme stress such as imprisonment, slavery, concentration camp, war experiences or even a long-term repressive, unhappy marriage — any stress in which the biochemical balance of the body is permanently damaged. When similar stressful circumstances are met in the present life, there is a reactivation of the former imbalanced pattern carried by the astral scar.

To heal the scar on the astral body, it is helpful to understand the former life situation that caused it and release the emotion connected to it. It is not entirely necessary to remember the cause. You can ask for the scar to be healed on the dream plane. Additionally, using chemical or herbal medications as an adjunct can help the physical body remember its true homeostasis and help break the pattern on all levels.

The patterning of depression from astral scarring extends beyond emotions and physical symptoms. The pattern is like a filter through which reality is perceived and life energies enter. Depression is a diminishing felt on all levels, which includes all forms of abundance, so that poverty would be part of the patterning, as would loneliness and isolation. The pattern resonating into the physical life from the astral scar suppresses all aspects as it moves through the bodies of consciousness to the physical level.

There are other aspects of depression that particularly affect walk-ins. One is connected to mourning and loss. Because Earth consciousness is so compartmentalized, some levels of consciousness feel a deep sense of loss and experience a period of mourning for the traits that walked out. There is also the fact that most walk-ins come from civilizations in which the ordinary state of mind would be considered bliss by Earth standards. Therefore, the ordinary Earth state would definitely be downward for them. It would require adjustments that necessitate learning to operate comfortably in the Earth state, then slowly bringing in the energy of joy they consider normal.

Walk-ins who move into a vehicle with this type of scarring will need to clear it before moving on to their own agenda. You might find that when certain life circumstances are encountered, this scar tissue will be irritated and reactivated. Like a tone that, when struck, will resonate in the higher octaves, a life event can trigger all the symptoms of the original scenario. A sensitive therapist who can assist with past-life access is very helpful. Sometimes not regarding this scar as your personal drama can remove self-judgment and self-condemnation, which are so prevalent in Earth-mode thinking. This will relieve one source of pain.

Your world is going through major changes. The breakdown between levels of consciousness can be used to your advantage in this type of situation. We cannot emphasize too strongly how much your dream plane serves your waking life. Giving your dreaming self problems that need to be solved can bring about a resolution that sometimes entirely bypasses the need to address it on the waking level.

Many walk-ins have skills at home that exceed present Earth abilities. Some skills can be brought onto this plane; others can never be used here. However, many of these abilities can be accessed on the dream level and can affect your living-plane reality through the dream route. Turn your problems over to the portion of yourself who is the dream master and find the best solutions.

FIFTEEN

Time and Prophecy in the Transitional Age

Grace

You are on the path of transmutation initiated by the return of the light energy to the Earth plane. This light energy is changing the vibrational rate of the Earth and it will change your perceptions of your world through the study of physics. Those at the head of the pack in adjusting to the changes are probably experiencing aberrations in their perceptions of time. Time is an aspect of the Earth game that allows for the perception of reality as a linear progression. This is an agreed-upon illusion taken on by all who choose to participate in Earth's dramas.

In addition, the nature of your consciousness does not allow operation on multidimensional levels by the living-plane consciousness, which deals with everyday life. Your "hardware" is simply not designed to handle multirealities through the consciousness that is focused on daily living.

Your dream plane has a freer range of consciousness and perceptions, which is why it uses symbolism to communicate information to the living plane. Symbols, by their very nature, carry multilayers of meanings. The living-plane consciousness can then unravel the meanings one by one and perceive them in a linear manner.

Changes are taking place in the basic structure of your physical vehicle that will allow you to handle more than one reality at a time. You are gaining greater abilities to shift to altered states of consciousness. At different levels you can access different realities, like turning the dial on a radio. You might begin to find you are capable of holding more than one "station" simultaneously in a flicker effect while the new dimensions of your brain blend the levels into one data flow. This is not unlike the type of channeling that is happening now. There is a blending of channeled consciousness with the host's various data banks to produce a single line of information.

As you move into the age of light, there are dramatic changes taking place that provide a spectrum of probable realities from which individuals can choose as they move into the future. Every event, from the most insignificant gesture of an individual to a major event on a worldwide scale, plays out every variation of its unfolding on some level of reality. The loosening of the tyranny of time is making it possible to jump the tracks from one reality to an alternate one with much greater facility than was previously possible.

The moving of Earth life into the age of light will reveal many who do not choose to participate in the transmutation involved. Those of you who are aware of the changes know that it is not easy. Clearing debris from the bodies of consciousness can be very painful. This is because bodies are taking in more light energy, which cannot occupy the same "space" with the dark or negative energies; like a barrel of oil, when you add more and more water to it, the oil will spill out. The "spilling" of negative energies from the bodies of consciousness plays out in the form of physical illness and emotional pain.

Many are choosing to leave this life now and return in another incarnation after the new world has stabilized. Others are choosing to stay in a probable reality in which the world continues on its present polarized path, avoiding dramatic change. In between these extremes there is a wide range of probable scenarios with different ratios of change and stasis.

This is why many individuals seem to be going in all different directions. In a single lifetime an individual might jump tracks of probable realities several times before settling on one line of progress into this new age.

Those among you who carry the gift of prophecy, whether as an intuitive guide in your personal life or as a profession, might be disturbed by fluctuations in your skills. This will pass. Allow for greater errors during the chaos of transition. You are learning new ways to sense time and are being confronted with more probability shifts than you have been used to. Sensing which line holds the highest energy for becoming the line of the living plane is a challenge you'll meet as your abilities expand. In light of such a joyful prospect, you will be moving into a new way of "reading" reality. Many of the reasons for scanning the future will no longer arise. This will occur naturally as suffering is left behind in the darkness and a joyful participation in life becomes the norm.

SIXTEEN

Healthy Expressions

Drumming: Adjunct to Healing and Transformation

White Crow

The use of percussive sound to communicate data transcends many forms of communication in a way that is both ancient and futuristic. It also surpasses some of the most sophisticated technologies. The elements involved in this simple procedure are the creation of a vibratory resonance, further defined by an assigned numerical pattern imbued with the consciousness of intent.

Drumming as it is practiced in all the cultures on your world has the capacity to communicate the consciousness of the drummer. The beats are not just empty sounds arranged in an interesting or exciting pattern. They are a vehicle for the consciousness of the one who strikes the beats. At the present time, except in some primitive cultures, this is mostly an unconscious phenomenon. However, there have been past cultures that understood the power available through this means of communication.

Drumming with a group aligns the individuals into an energy unit through the vibration of the beats. If that unit is evoking a particular intent, there is a tremendous power generated. Many cultures you consider primitive have been using this power for thousands of years.

This ancient technology can be applied to healing procedures by regarding the human body as the drum. By lightly tapping beats on the surface of the skin, you can affect the aspects of the body beneath the skin and the effects will ripple out to the bodies of consciousness connected to the point of percussion.

The numerical patterns of the beats have an alignment with the study of numerology and the characteristics of the numbers. There are different responses to binary or tertiary rhythms and odd or even meters. Generally speaking, binary rhythms, like 2/4 or 4/4, are very grounding. Their emphasis is downward. A three rhythm such as a waltz (3/4) has a swinging or circular feeling. It resonates more with the emotional body of consciousness. Rhythms that have an upbeat ("and-*1*") pull you away from the ground; they are uplifting. The beat of the human heart is an upbeat. This is the inner rhythm you live with all the time.

As to odd meters like 5/8 or 7/8, you can try kinesiology (muscle-testing) while these are being tapped. You might find that some patterns produce a muscle weakness when tapped at certain points and at other points will strengthen and balance the body energies. In general, these odd rhythms are more likely to be activating in their effect. There is a sense of driving the beat, a feeling of propulsion in their patterns.

Rhythms can open and stimulate chakra activity or release and balance energy in an area of pain or sickness by tapping them out lightly on the body. You might differentiate the meters (2/4, 3/4 and so on) by accenting the first beat or by alternating your hands, using one hand to tap the first beat and the other for the rest of the pattern.

There are many elements you can experiment with. You are dealing with all the qualities inherent in numerology, the chakras, right and left hands, parts of the body that express illness or pain and what they represent in terms of emotional connections and mental beliefs. In addition, there are the effects of sonics and resonance applied to the physical body and the very important consciousness and intent of the drummer. As you experiment with these elements, you will evolve your own techniques for their use.

[A word of caution: When using the tapping for activation, a detoxification process can be stimulated involving the bodies of consciousness. The reactions might vary from one individual to another according to where each individual is in his/her transformation process.]

Dancing and the Custodians of the Dance

Hannah Beaconsfield

There was a sacred level of human consciousness in prehistoric (and current primitive) societies that operated through ceremonies of human movement and generated powerful energy for the use of the community. This energy generator is called dance. The nature of the energy was based on communal needs and requests.

The Western development of complex societies, which evolved into vast bureaucratic civilizations driven by a male-dominated world consciousness, divided the sacred and the secular aspects of life into two separate endeavors. As the bureaucratic consciousness divided the integrated tribal spirit into compartments, the arts became designated as feminine endeavors. Every human expression that was defined by feminine qualities grew to have less and less value as the female herself lost more and more status. Of all the arts, the one designated as the most female-aligned — and the least valued — was dance.

In the sacred/secular split, dance was cast to the secular side. It was, after all, the art that used the body as its instrument of expression. Given the masculine-bound viewpoint of what was and was not sacred, the descent of dance from secular to profane was inevitable. For centuries dance served the secular by allowing the social interaction of young males and females in order to bond and form new families. It served the profane by encouraging women to display erotic movement to inflame masculine desires. Only if dance served the skills of battle did men own it. Although these are valid expressions, dance in its sacred form was lost.

Having been given to the custody of women, dance limped along behind the other fine arts as an artistic expression. Dance has periodically reached heights of exquisite artistry while in their custody. But in a society with priests and few priestesses, dance has never been given the support that was given music and painting. Only with the return of female energy in the form of the priestess could dance once again express the sacred.

In preparation for Earth's transformation to an integrated light planet, the twentieth century has witnessed the return of the priestess in the field of dance. A phenomenon has occurred that has no precedent in known world history. Several women of great creative brilliance, even genius, have reached levels of accomplishment and fame in the art of choreography and dance. One might be a fluke, but several is a movement. They are not only brilliant but influential. They have had a powerful effect on our entire modern sensibilities. The priestess energy is back!

Who are these women? Isadora Duncan, Ruth St. Denis, Doris Humphrey, Mary Wigman and the acknowledged high priestess, Martha Graham. Each of these priestesses created a lineage through their acolytes of the highest levels of expression of what it means to be a sacred human on this world. Even if you are not familiar with the art of dance and these names, you can be assured that their energy is flowing through the mass consciousness, awakening the priestess element in each person to complement and integrate with the established priest energy and form a new sense of the sacred in an enlightened world consciousness.

The Dance of Metamorphosis

White Crow

After the exuberance of childhood, most people in your highly civilized national cultures have been conditioned to restrain any spontaneous outbursts of expressive movement. In order to rediscover the free expression of childhood, you need to put a conscious effort into this endeavor. The body that is allowed a free expression through rhythmic movement automatically integrates the divided aspects of the total self. When you allow the body to express itself without self-consciousness, the smooth flow of left/right physical coordination is integrated with the other bodies of consciousness.

Dance classes give you a sense of confidence that your body can express itself beyond the mundane level of movement, and they are very valuable in assisting you with many aspects of your transformation process. Such classes strengthen the physical aspects of the body — not just the muscles, but the total functioning of the organs, glands and the release of toxins. This helps ease many physical complaints of transformation. Any vigorous exercise can do this, but dance engages much more of the total self.

Dance wonderfully supports many elements of the metamorphosis your human species is undergoing at this time of your dimensional ascension. Dance allows the emotional body to express the feelings that are flowing and release blocked feelings. The mental processes that integrate the two hemispheres of the brain are activated by the coordinated movement of free expression as well as by learning set dance sequences. And the rhythmic movement to music and/or drumbeats has the power to expand the consciousness and engage the spirit, giving it a vehicle for expression on this world.

SEVENTEEN

The Feminine Factor in Prophecy

The Pleiadian Light

The elusive nature of prophecy at the present time is due to the high level of chaos that occurs at periods of dramatic change. As you are aware, there is always a breaking down of old patterns before new structures can be created. In addition to this basic pattern of change, there is another factor emerging at this juncture of the Earth's evolution. This is the rise of the feminine energy.

All the feminine elements of the life force and all the characteristics that you have assigned to the feminine portion of this world's polarity are returning to a position of power. They have been in a recessive or latent position for eons. This feminine polarity is not returning to an ascendancy over the present male-dominant culture as it has in periods in your past. The feminine energy is returning to integrate with the masculine energy from a position of equal power. The integration of these two threads will weave a fabric that will form an entirely new garment of characteristics to be worn by the world consciousness as it moves into the age of light.

Another analogy we could give to represent this blending would be to liken it to a river, an ancient river flowing on a predictable path. If you are at one point on the river and wish to predict what is around the next bend, you need only your innate intuition and some knowledge of both the terrain and the nature of water. With this information you are able to predict the river's path with varying degrees of accuracy.

However, if a tributary feeding the river opened up with an equal force and merged with it, the once-predictable path could no longer be gauged so easily. The force of the merged energies could cause any number of changes in the path of flow. It would certainly spread out over more land. The incoming force could cause the river to veer and churn its way through an entirely new route. It could even divide into multiple smaller rivers, as in a delta. This is how the return of the feminine energy as an equal force will affect your future.

We are aware of many prophets on your plane presenting their visions of the future. Some are very skilled and can accurately see a specific future evolving from their present point. However, the return of the feminine energy is a wild card that many seers are not taking into account, even on intuitive levels.

It is very hard to predict a future event when it involves a circumstance that your world has never experienced: the true balance and integration of the energies that represent male and female. Understand that we are not referring to the genders of your physical bodies, though those who are living through female bodies are now moving into social and economic positions that give them more power. This is the *result* of the return of the feminine energy rather than its cause.

We are speaking of the qualities carried by the receptive aspect of the Earth psyche, which is contained in both genders. These qualities include evolution rather than revolution; cooperation rather than competition; allowing rather than controlling; nurturing rather than consuming; peace rather than war; "with" instead of "against."

Shuffle these cards into your fortunetelling deck and you will find you are playing with a whole new potential for the Earth-human future. The events created by such a mass consciousness will be very different from the present polarized point of progression, so different that it's hard for you to imagine, let alone predict its future events. When you factor in this integration, you will be more accurate in your predictions.

This integration process is occurring on a minute-by-minute

basis on your world. Your awareness and recognition of these new values will assist in speeding and accommodating the transition. This integration is happening within your individual psyches as well as the consciousness of Earth humanity as a whole. Encouraging the process within yourself first will add your weight to the integration of the collective psyche on your world.

EIGHTEEN

Shepherding the Fragments of the Self

The Pleiadian Light

Due to the stratified nature of Earth-plane consciousness, there is the potential for fragmentation of the self in response to life events. It is the nature of your world to confine different aspects of your consciousness in different compartments. If you could view your consciousness from a broad overview, you would be amazed to see how it is comprised of self-contained units that form a mosaic of the identity you recognize as yourself.

This fractured pattern also serves the unconscious in dealing with life experiences that have powerful energy/emotions attached to them. When a life circumstance cannot be handled by the living-plane consciousness, sometimes the choice is to break off a fragment of the psyche to preserve the integrity of the whole. Fragments of consciousness can split off and become locked into a "time point" like a loop of film that replays an action over and over. The causes for this fragmentation can be traumas or attachments so strong that a fragment must be left behind so that the life can progress. For walk-ins and all who are working on their metaphysical growth, these fragments often need attention and reintegration before further progress can be made.

In the case of trauma, it is the inability of the total consciousness to live with the event that causes a portion to be left behind. In the case of attachments, it is the inability to live without the valued time point that creates a fragment. Traumas cause the most problems; attachments aren't usually bothersome unless they are holding you back.

Walk-ins will need to lead any detached fragments from the life of the original occupant to reintegrate with their spirit, which has moved on. This can be done on the dream plane. You can simply ask that you meet on the dream plane with spiritual guides who will help you gather the fragments together and lead them into the light to reintegrate with their source.

Lightworkers who are processing fragmentation from their past can use the same process. They will be reintegrating their own spirit level of consciousness. The integrity that results from this work can spontaneously release old painful patterns and allow a new energy flow to propel the life forward.

NINETEEN

Dolphins in New York

A Dolphin Trio

There was a news report that dolphins were sighted in New York City's East River [March 13, 1997]. I asked for information on this, and the Pleiadian Light first responded.

The sighting of dolphins in the East River is indeed accurate. They have voluntarily taken on the physical water environment and the New York City vibratory energy for a particular purpose. The expedition is made up of three dolphins: one male, two females. Their mission has been to provide energetic support for the United Nations during a period of threat to both the physical establishment and the world organization as a whole.

The dolphins as well as the whales represent a sentient species of Sirius energy on Earth. They and other extraterrestrial support teams place great hope in the United Nations as a unifier of your world energy and as a vehicle to act as a clearinghouse for intergalactic interactions on this world.

Could I channel the dolphins, and would they give a name?

This is dolphin, male, no name. We are a triadic energy unit. If you need a designation, you may choose one. Use something like three, trio, triangle — a word that resonates that energy.

May I call you "Pod de trois"?

Yes, we love that. It does capture our energy and our spirit in one phrase.

Is there any particular information you would like to channel right now?

We would like your human world consciousness to know that the Sirius energy radiating from our home base is coming in force to assist your transformation at this time. The cetacean species in your world waters are acting like grounding agents for both the activating energies and the spirit of integration that Sirius represents. The Sirius energy participated in your inception as a polarized world consciousness, and is now returning to participate in your inception as an integrated consciousness.

By living with you, we, the dolphin and whale cohabitants of Earth, are in a good position to assist your evolution into the intergalactic community. We are alien creatures among you; yet you regard us as your own and appreciate our intelligence and compassion, not to mention our gymnastic and theatrical abilities.

Because of our nature our messages often translate as humor. We just can't become too ponderous about all these changes. Speaking of ponderous, we could actually have used some whale energy on this U.N. mission, some big guns. But we didn't know anyone who could fit through the inlet without setting off a war between the professional preservationists and the last vestiges of the hunter/provider mentality on your plane — not to mention the uproar in the tabloid press.

So the three of us got the assignment. If the human world can be helped by two or three aquatic comics, we are doing our best to spread *light*-hearted energy to support the en*light*enment of the Earth-human species.

What can we Earth folk do to take advantage of your presence and your assistance?

Well, it would help if you stopped trying to wipe out our species, but aside from that, use any means to match up your individual vibratory rate with ours. There are many places now where you can interact with our physical presence, even swim in the ocean with us. We voluntarily participate in theatrical water shows, not just because it's a lot of fun and we love the applause, but because there are powerful energy interactions between us and the audience. It allows a lot of people to get to know us and love us. What you love you align with. Even seeing those shows on TV has a powerful effect.

Those who are not in a position to be in our presence physically can bring a dolphin or whale image into their energy sphere, and their vibratory patterns will be altered simply by an awareness of the presence of a token representing our image. This could be a piece of jewelry or a keychain, something you keep close to your person.

The energies you will be aligning with support many of the patterns of fourth-density reality to which you are ascending. If you study our life form, our family units and communities, our forms of communication, our delight in life and our playful approach to it, you will get a glimpse of the quality, if not the species, of your life in the future. No, it is not the meek, but the *clowns* who will inherit the Earth!

TWENTY

The Promise of the Caduceus

Nordestera

Nordestera is an energy/information source from the integrated light level of Sirius.

We are an energy that resonates the vibration of the Sirius global consciousness. We will give you the name Nordestera to identify us. This is a vibrational conversion, not a true appellation that we carry or use. It is for your convenience that we present a title for ourselves.

The energy of the Sirius consciousness was one of the contributors to the creation of the Earth world. We not only added our input to the humanoid expression on your world, but assisted in creating and developing many of the animal species as well. The Sirius influence on earthly human development was not a physical seeding, as was the case with other extraterrestrial groups. It was a frequency of consciousness that we contributed, not physical genetic material. However, this pattern of consciousness contributed some formational effects on physical development.

It was the Earth's unconscious that was defined or seeded by this frequency. We are referring to the portion of Earth consciousness that you call subconscious. For the purpose of clarity let us define *unconscious* as a vast metaphysical domain that contains the full range of realities you cannot perceive from your present third-dimensional position. *Subconscious* will represent the range of Earth realities that are not available to your conscious perceptions.

You might say we contributed to the anatomy of the fragment of Earth's consciousness that lies beneath surface awareness. What we planted in this fragment were seeds of consciousness that could not germinate until certain conditions were available to support their growth.

The Sirius energy is an energy of balance and resonates with the process of integration. The seeds of Sirius could not germinate in a global consciousness that plays out the dramas of polarity, going deeper and deeper into separation. Only now as the darkness of separation is ending and the sparks of integration are becoming visible can the Sirius energy return.

There are two mythic images carried in your global subconscious that in some aspects have held the promise of this return: the snake and the bird. Many of the Sirius-related images combine these into one image. The *caduceus*, the symbol carried by the medical community, is one such image. Of course, this is not a coincidence but a true reflection of Sirius' support for the healing of human misery. These mythic images are the dream symbols that rose from the human subconscious to remind you of your Sirius connections. Even more important, they hold the promise of a return to an integrated state and the healing of humankind through balance.

In the case of the caduceus, the two snakes represent the double helix — the third-density level of the staff of Earth life. The wings hold the promise of the ascension that humankind is now approaching. The Sirius energy is returning in large vibratory waves now, heralding the transformation of the serpent into the bird — or, more accurately, the true integration of the serpent and the bird.

The integration of the caduceus is the integration of the elements of the subconscious. The reptile and the winged creature are divisions in symbols (the language of the subconscious) of negative and positive, dark and light, of all polarities as they play out in the subconscious terrain. The influences of Sirius on your plane have also appeared as fearful reptilian creatures and loving winged beings. For at your level of separation, you can view us only in our separated aspects. Both these aspects represent our energy at a past point of separation; however, our approach to you now is from our integrated position.

We, Nordestera, represent the ascended, or winged, aspect of Sirius. Our energy also resonates as angelic in your understanding. Some of the winged visions you hold and depict through images represent an angelic level of our global consciousness. They also represent the future angelic level of your own development. With the integration of our energy as one of your returning parents, along with energies of other extraterrestrials, you are attaining a level of consciousness as if your bodies had wings to fly high and perceive much more of the terrain of reality.

The bird species on your planet offer you an opportunity to use them as a stencil by observing, appreciating and aligning with them. The cultivation of this type of relationship with birds will help you entrain your vibrations with some genetic characteristics birds carry that are similar to characteristics unfolding in the expansion of your consciousness.

Examples would be all those characteristics aligned with pineal activity and the awakening of the complex activities of the limbic system of the brain. Birds have a much higher ratio of pineal to brain size than that of humans. In addition, they have a flattened cranium that brings the pineal closer to the surface so it can receive stimulation from sunlight. Many exotic birds actually drop crown feathers to expose a patch of bare skin to the activating effects of light.

The pineal is aligned with the third-eye chakra and actually has some cellular similarities to a physical eye. It is stimulated by light — both physical light and the enlightenment of the species. The pineal gland in humans, even before it atrophies with age, is a minuscule portion of the brain. In the evolving human species the pineal gland and the limbic system will constitute the dominant glandular center in the brain. It will replace the pituitary as the master gland. The pituitary has served as master of the glandular activity in the third-dimensional version of the physical body.

The master gland for a lighter body, a less dense physical reality, will need the support of the limbic system, which involves the integration of information from various senses, systems and brain activities. It has additional characteristics at a latent level that you will not be able to perceive or understand until that glandular and energetic center is activated to discern them.

The bird energy also carries many symbolic meanings dear to the emotional and spiritual levels of self. The capacity for flight holds a promise of freedom from many of the burdens that weigh down third-density physical life. There are also the elements of the dove of peace and the God energy in the form of the Holy Spirit that are aligned with the elements of integration and ascension.

When our energy, as the Sirius contributors to the birth of the earthly consciousness, withdrew to allow you to go through your growing pains, we left a promise of our return encoded deep in your mass subconscious. You have reminded yourselves of this promise by surfacing mythic symbols like the caduceus that appear from time to time. You will find these symbolic elements in many different cultures throughout your history.

And now we are keeping our promise. We are returning on wings of powerful energy to assist your emergence into the adulthood of your world species. We are returning to help you to fly free, to ascend.

TWENTY-ONE

What Do We Do with the Warriors?

Nordestera

We wish to address the link between the dark energies of destruction and the warrior spirit that has helped to create your world culture. Many present at this time have had either past-life experiences operating in dark energy or as warriors trained for battle — or even both in the same individual.

Understanding that you wish to resolve these past lives at this time of integration and transformation, we ask that for the moment you regard the dark energies free from their effects as energy in action causing havoc, cruelty and destruction. Recognize them simply as energy sources that have been traditionally expressed in a specific way. Also understand that the warrior spirit is such a deeply held archetype that its natural impulse, when confronted by any challenge, evokes that spirit to take charge.

In your world history, past and present, the images of the warrior and the dark energies have often become superimposed. As you move into your transformation there is a two-pronged challenge that needs to be addressed by lightworking individuals and your masculine warrior-world consciousness.

You can beat the swords into plowshares, but what do you do with the warriors? There is no simple answer, for it is a process. The warrior energy has served the survival of the individual and the species on your physical plane of polarities. Therefore it must be graduated to other energy expressions.

You have transitional methods in place, and using them consciously would be very helpful. They are your games and sports. There has been a shifting in this century to include not only warlike team competitions but the individual athlete as a warrior against the limitations of the physical body in a physical-world circumstance. This is a step toward the integration of the energy that has supported battle.

The vicarious participation in all sorts of sports and competitive events is a valuable conversion for the energy that the species has put into warfare. This vicarious interest will gradually shift in many different directions, dispersing the destructive aspect of the energy.

As for the dark, negative energies of wanton destruction that you designate as evil, it is easy to see how these energies would take advantage of the warrior and feed off the energy of battle. The first step in dealing with this link is to disengage the conscious connections between the warrior and the dark-energy expressions. The positive attitude toward the warrior spirit that has defended the species distorts the ability to perceive the negative energies of destruction.

Both of these forces must be integrated on your world in order to ascend to your next level of growth. The warrior must be integrated because the role does not serve the future and has no place in it. The dark energies must be integrated because they represent the polar aspects of your total reality that are denied, reviled and cast out. Their disenfranchisement from what you define as human/humane has left them to grow and flourish like a hidden fungus in a dark, damp pocket of your world reality, feeding on necrotic matter and needing more and more of it to survive.

Recognizing that they are simply the other side of the coin of your polarized reality is sometimes difficult. However, recognition and acknowledgment allows integration. A fungus is just another life form when viewing the full spectrum.

Now that we have inserted a wedge between the warrior and evil forces, we would like to present some suggestions as to how an individual can resolve negative influences in the present and/or those carried over from other lifetimes. One way is to track down each life through past-life regression and create an alternate life in which a different course was taken. This procedure takes some time. This siphons off some of the energy of negativity in the previous life. Perhaps it is more correct to say that this tunes in to an alternate life, because every potential for the unfolding of a life already exists as a probability.

Another way you can neutralize the negative energies from a series of past lives is to create a vision in which you gather all these other selves together. Speak to them in a loving manner and reassure them that they are valued and will not lose their identities, but that now it is time to go home. You will be taking them to integrate with your soul family on its level of integrated light. As they reenter the soul family they are embraced by the integrated energy and all negativity connected to them is neutralized.

Or you might envision a scenario in which you escort them onto a plane or craft of some kind and fly it yourself, taking them home. Do not be surprised that even though it is your vision, some of them might resist, for fear is the energy they have lived on. Visualize the home you take them to as a magnificent building that radiates light. You might have to repeat this procedure until you are sure all of the flock is safely home.

We have presented two different approaches to this process. You can also take the ideas and create your own scenarios. The important thing is to integrate their energy with the total soul-self and neutralize the negativity. Offering loving support for these fragments is the best thing you can do, no matter what visualized course of action you construct. Please understand that the drama you construct is just as real on another level of consciousness as your present day-to-day life; it has just as much power to effect changes.

TWENTY-TWO

An Open Letter to Healers

Grace

Your world views disease as an enemy that you must fight. Noble healing warriors have been taking up the sword against disease for centuries. However, the time of the sword is coming to an end. Your world is beginning to grasp that wars do not solve anything. Whatever you attack simply goes to even greater lengths to fight against you.

This is the beginning of the time of integration. Your warrior spirits will begin merging the attack impulse with the defend impulse into an unnamed energy that provides aggressive nurturing. Understand that these are attempts on our part to translate powerful energy concepts into limited verbal definitions.

You have already witnessed the defenses of disease microbes against the deadly chemicals aimed at them. They respond by mutating into new versions of themselves that are resistant to the chemical attacks. The consciousness of diametric opposition, which is the substructure of polarized world cultures, uses conflict to seek balance.

Polarization is an illusion. Unity is truth, or as close to the concept as you can accommodate. World cultures are polarized to learn lessons, to gain experience and enrich the total deity level of consciousness — the I Am or God source. The world culture will return home with these gifts, reintegrating with Source.

We would suggest to all healers that you break the warrior's sword. Open yourselves to perceiving the elements of the patient/client that are whole, balanced, healthy and shining with light. No matter how small, there is some fragment of this light energy in even the most seriously ill person imaginable. Aggressively nurturing this fragment is the healing of the future rather than fighting the disease.

The very best healers can do for their patients is to view them from a transcendent perspective — that they are absolutely perfect the way they are. In truth, they *are* a perfect evolution of themselves as they utilize their individual skills in their world situation. Viewing patients as perfect is a more realistic perception and supports the portion of patients that use all the available opportunities, including illness, to fulfill the larger agenda. This has brought them to a place that makes use of one form of illness or another as a problem-solving mechanism.

The next step is to open yourselves intuitively to what your patient's agenda is. Even if you grasp this only in a sense of abstract patterns and energy flows, you are in a position to assist the patient in finding paths to alternate solutions that will serve just as well in the long run and are more comfortable.

The inability of your world to view the full scope of an individual's consciousness patterns causes you to perceive what you call illness as something wrong. The truth might be that the illness is the best possible solution for the agenda of the total self.

Do remember, we only make suggestions. You will find the best ways to use your gifts for yourselves. We wish you to understand that our energy is also available. In representing the female archetype of the christed woman, we are the emerging half of your polarized energy, which will integrate to alter the nature of reality in the age of light.

TWENTY-THREE

The Value of Hope

Grace

Hope is a concept created by Earth inhabitants. It is based on the belief in a linear time flow. This concept was a very clever creation, for Earth life is a game of challenges. Many of these challenges can be so difficult and painful that there would be little inducement to stay if you couldn't project beyond the present to a happier circumstance.

Regarding adjusting to the new age, there is a great deal of advice about learning to live in the moment. To the native Earth dwellers as well as walk-ins, the concept of living in the moment can be difficult to hold. Much of daily life on Earth depends on time references. You make an appointment for next week; you realize you forgot a friend's birthday last week; you look at your watch to make sure you'll catch your train. The awareness of time is built into every moment of the most prosaic day on Earth.

Practicing living in the moment is valuable in preparing for the evolution that is under way. In this period of change time is condensing. You are on the path of return to the vortex of energy that is the still point of the moment.

For some walk-ins this transition can present a problem point in their journey. This is because they are bringing in their sense of timelessness before their living-plane consciousness, programmed by the original occupant, can handle it.

As a walk-in becomes adjusted and begins to bring in his/her skills and perceptions of reality, her sense of past and future begins to diminish. She is moving into living in the moment, which is a natural state for her. However, there might be residual problems in the life she has taken on.

For the natural-born Earth dweller the transition from linear time to living in the moment will occur gradually. Before a person realizes that he has lost hope by moving into the moment, he can become disoriented. It becomes apparent how valuable hope is, because a future vision can be created in which his problems are resolved, easing the discomfort of the present. It gives him hope.

In this time of transition hope is still valuable even if it keeps you in linear time. Hope is a benevolent creation. It is a valuable gift for as long as you need it.

PART 3

EXTRATERRESTRIAL CONNECTIONS

TWENTY-FOUR

The Intergalactic Peace Corps

The Pleiadian Light

Many replacement spirits taking over Earth bodies are counterparts from ET civilizations. This is not an "invasion of the body snatchers." (However, that movie scenario did purge a lot of fears in preparation for the influx of alien energy.) The alien energy coming onto the Earth plane now is more like your Peace Corps. ET individuals give their time and expertise to assist this world in taking a major step toward being an intergalactic player.

As you have seen in the walk-in account presented here, the ET peace-corps participants have to make adjustments to working in foreign territory. Because forgetfulness to one degree or another is part of the conditions on Earth, it helps to have some idea of what ET influences are bringing to this world.

A large source of walk-in energy to this world has been Pleiadian. However, the new influx of walk-ins has a high level of Sirian energy. Sirius has figured strongly in Earth history, particularly in the Egyptian heritage, which is one of the foundation blocks for Western civilization.

The Sirian energy has maintained a presence on Earth in the form of whales and dolphins. The cetaceans on this planet are physically comparable to humanoids and are self-aware and self-determining just as the humans are. You might say they are a technology-free sentient species that on many levels is more advanced than humans.

Since the Sirian walk-in energy is similar to the dolphins in their approach to life, it has a particular affinity for the cetaceans. Their energies support the healing arts, the integration of polarities and, with that integration, the return of the feminine force as an equal power on this world.

[To understand the spectrum of ET influence on Earth and its evolution, I recommend a book that presents this material and was born a classic: *The Prism of Lyra* by Lyssa Royal-Holt and Keith Priest.]

TWENTY-FIVE

Introduction to the Metaphysics of Contact

The Pleiadian Light

We give you our Pleiadian greeting, which holds wishes for your evolution into a species that is capable of sustaining peace. In your world this means the balance achieved by the integration of polarities. And we wish a joyful emotional support for all your endeavors. The spirit of joy is by its nature uplifting and expansive. This resonates with the process of transformation/ascension that your planet is experiencing. In a nutshell, we support all your growth endeavors by wishing you peace and joy.

On another very important level we give you this greeting to make it clear that our intent in contacting your world is peaceful. We open channelings with this greeting to help calm some of your fears connected with alien invasions.

Your third-dimensional world has fear built into its basic DNA structure as a survival tool. Therefore, fear is one of the major barriers to open contact with your world. Even those who are very excited about opening intergalactic communication and have been preparing for it through study and practice would be overwhelmed with a fright/flight response at confronting on your front lawn a craft, ET visitors and the energy they resonate. Dealing with this automatic reaction is one of the considerations you have to face and one the ETs must understand.

There are several organizations on your world that are responsibly undertaking projects intended to initiate contact and establish lines of communication. The ETs working with these projects understand what is expected of them and are cooperating with the Earth communicators. These projects involve limited contact events such as light signals, sounds and the energy of presence. This is to help you document and share information that is not too dramatic in order to prevent overreactions that are either pro or con.

We would like to add, perhaps deepening your trust in ET contact, that many interactions you believe are with angels are with our energy. Your world is definitely experiencing angelic interventions, but some of the interactions are with benevolent ET entities.

The area we would like to address in the multilevel project of opening contact with other worlds is the area of metaphysics involved in the meeting of alien worlds. Many die-hard, lifelong UFO/alien life-form researchers have not given consideration to the aspects of ET contact that lie beyond recordable documentation and the long-hoped-for face-to-face handshake.

From our perspective, this is the last and, to a large degree, the least important step of the contact scenario. We wish to consider the *meta* ("beyond or transcendent") and the *physics* (the study of the physical world) aspects of making contact possible. We will give you a little analogy because a simple mental picture can contain volumes within it: You are like a small child (we don't choose this image to demean you in any way) who wishes to open a door to a room where the grownups are having a party. However, you are too small to reach the doorknob.

Some circumstances must change for you to accomplish what you desire. You might look for objects to pile near the door and climb on to reach the knob. Or you could wait until you grow large enough to reach the knob or until a combination of circumstances might be a more appropriate solution. Or you can combine the last two: allow time for growth and simultaneously create some inspired, inventive steps to reach your goal — playing with the big kids — in the intergalactic arena.

The level that you *can't* reach translates to the level of consciousness of the ET cultures with whom you wish to interact. Almost all ETs working on the Earth project right now are on evolutionary levels beyond yours. Given that your planetary level is third-dimensional, those working with you are fourth- and fifth-dimensional planetary species or interdimensional energies operating beyond the physical level of the culture such as we are. We represent the integrated level of the Pleiadian world consciousness. You are also receiving guidance and supportful interaction from interdimensional energies who have never been part of a physical world, like angels.

Understand that we use numerical designations to translate our information; however, we feel there are elements of illusion in them. This is because your stratified world likes to use numbers to designate better-than or worse-than. All is equal; the different levels are like colors, no one better than another. But all combine to make a rainbow.

We are not denying that there are negative or dark energies connected to otherworld cultures. These energies previously and presently have tried interacting with your plane. But because you have begun your journey into the age of light, this is a path that the dark energies don't even recognize, and you are literally moving beyond their perception. You are visible to energies at or above your level, so you can set that fear aside and keep moving ahead.

We will discuss four metaphysical concepts that hold some of the greatest dichotomies for both yourselves and for the ETs working toward contact.

Spiritual Development

When we use the term "spiritual development" in channeling to many on the Earth plane, we perceive a retraction of energy — a withdrawing from the idea. This, we sense, has to do with your associating the term with organized religions on your world. Those who have had negative experiences in their church connections recoil from the words "spiritual development." It encapsulates ideas of repression of many activities considered pleasurable.

For those who have found comfort and support from organized religion, we experience another difficulty. There is often a suspicion that ETs, no matter how spiritually oriented, pose a threat to belief in the God concepts of particular sects. To us the development of the spirit supports the portion of ourselves that is the energy of God within that unifies us. We are all fragments of Source/All That Is/God. This spirit portion exists at all times at a level of joyfulness that can't even be imagined by those caught between the negative and the positive of a polarized reality.

There are many humanoid species in planetary lives whose world consciousness is utopian by your standards. If we say that these utopian cultures live at high levels of spiritual development, many of you would equate this as being no fun. There is a feeling that fun is aligned with going against culturally repressive restraints. This is a polarity-bound idea. When you see that integration provides all the enjoyments you felt you were denied in a polarized world, it will be "cool" to be part of a spiritually developed utopian world culture.

Right now as you reach for ET connections, consider the metaphysical concepts to which we refer and the focus on growth of the spirit to be simply how it is for ET groups. If you wish to open communication, you need to learn the language of those with whom you wish to speak. The language of the contacting ET groups is built on the consciousness of spirit.

Part of your dream of making contact with other worlds is the belief that you will gain from them information that will carry your technological development to powerful new heights. We would like for you to understand that higher technologies are built on the expansion of consciousness. The next evolutionary step in a technology based on physics is the evolution and integration of the *technology of consciousness.* This involves the expansion of perceptions to take in portions of the self that are beyond the physical. You could say it is the technology of spirit.

How do you learn the language of spirit and experience the expansion of consciousness? Simply by listening to, validating and supporting your own spiritual aspects. The first step in this is meditation. You must quiet the outside world from time to time to hear the inner world, which speaks in a softer voice.

The Nature of Time

In your world there are many illusions that join to form the world you recognize as real. One of these illusions is your concept of time. Outside of your own time/space world, time is not experienced in the same way. It is an element that can be invoked for different purposes by ET cultures that wish to use or work with the aspect of time, but it is elective. Beyond planetary living in physical bodies, time does not exist at all; there is only the eternal now. All reality is simultaneous. This concept is difficult to fully accommodate when you are working through a dense vehicle designed to filter reality into linear segments.

The ETs who are operating from less dense levels and experience a different sense of time can make adjustments in dealing with you. They have in their historical data banks the experience of having been third-dimensional and therefore understand how you operate. You, on the other hand, do not have in your day-to-day waking world the experience of temporal variations or nontime realities. But you do have imagination and intuition. These can assist you in adjusting your attitudes about contact, in terms of your need to have a time frame to work with.

The ETs understand your use of time and try to accommodate you when you ask for time frames for the contact scenario. You can help the process by understanding that for the ETs, things happen when they happen. When all the elements converge to produce a phenomenon, it is the right "time" for it to happen. This is the reverse of your belief that you must set a schedule or a goal, then proceed to do everything to make sure that your plan unfolds. If you hold this understanding of your different positions, you will ease your own apprehensions and support the way the ETs perceive the scenario.

Probable Realities

The concept of probable realities rests to a degree on your perception of time. In the multidimensional nature of the eternal now (all realities occurring simultaneously), every event that you perceive in linear time plays out every possible variation of itself on multilevels. You can perceive only one variation of the event in linear time. So for you the perceived variation is the "real" one. However, all other possible variations of how an event *could* unfold, *will and do* unfold, and are just as real in other dimensions.

In other words, at any still point in your concept of time, the possible lines of progress shoot out in all directions like an infinitely multipointed star. Each point represents a direction of progress that can be chosen. In this multipoint model all paths progress into their own reality. The individualized consciousness chooses one path and follows that reality. However, the multidimensional nature of your spirit consciousness creates an aspect of itself on *every* path at every point. Each path has a you on it — a you that is participating in each probable drama.

Your physical computer through which you are perceiving reality simply does not have the capacity to hold multireality programs. Your computer is designed to perceive only one line, one path of living progress. As you are living your linear-time life, these probabilities are of little consideration. However, when you project the future, you are really seeking the probability that has the highest energy level to support it. Until that probability is fully manifested on your plane, there could always be a shift in the energies to support an alternate probable reality.

We are working to clarify some of these concepts because they are often referred to in channeled material about the unfolding contact drama and are crucial to understanding how to bring about contact.

Multilevel Incarnational Lives

The concept of reincarnation is a linear-time-based interpretation of spirits taking up residence in physical bodies. It views the "residences" as occurring in a progressive manner. Understanding the concept of simultaneous time allows you to perceive incarnational lifetimes as not just linear, but also parallel and probable.

We are presenting this so you can understand that the ETs who are reaching to make contact are really aspects of yourselves. You can literally have an incarnational aspect of yourself (a simultaneous self from a concurrent otherworld reality) or a future self project into a simultaneous position in order to make contact with you — and many other variations as well.

Since you are not only preparing for ET contact at this time but also undergoing a planetary metamorphosis, all of these concepts that are the way it is for ETs will also be the way it is for you. World transformation and contacting other worlds go hand in hand, as does the study of metaphysics and the expansion of consciousness. You cannot open contact without opening consciousness. That's just the way it is!

TWENTY-SIX

Some Fine Points of Opening Contact

The Pleiadian Light

The groups on your world who are interested in UFOs and alien contact have many questions about when, where and how open contact will come about. We would like to present our perspective on the situation.

We don't see anything preventing or hindering face-to-face contact with us and other intergalactic civilizations. Some variables must be aligned before contact is possible. The variables we speak of are due to the wide range of characteristics and expressions of humanity on your world. There is no single cohesive world consciousness. The diversity on your plane is matched by few other worlds, so we approach the opening of contact in many ways and on many levels.

Your world is becoming more integrated, and the greater the knowledge you have of your own parts and the more you interact as an integrated world body, the easier you make it for other worlds to connect with you. Your world is doing that and changes are happening every day. This is why we cannot lay out a game plan for contact with you. Your world consciousness is like fireworks. Just when we think we have a clear view of your structure and brilliance, there is a colorful starburst from the center that changes everything.

This does not mean that individual and small group contacts can't happen. They *are* happening; and the accumulation of data from these incidents will push your world consciousness into common recognition of ET reality.

Another variable is the nature of consciousness experienced on the Earth plane. Your levels of consciousness are broken up into segregated sections. It is necessary to understand the reason Earth humans have established powerful barriers between levels of consciousness.

These barriers contribute to surviving in a world that has challenges so traumatic that they must be encapsulated and removed from conscious awareness in order for the being who experienced it to keep going and stay alive. This includes everything that comes under the definition of repression or denial as well as the perception of other realities that would be labeled psychotic. So when you are asking that these barriers be let down, there is a resistance on a basic level that believes the walls must stay up to preserve the capacity to function within the norm of your world.

These barriers also prevent you from perceiving realities that would be too jarring to your psyches or that do not fit into your belief systems. This includes alien craft and their humanoid species. Though many Earth humans are shifting their belief systems, allowing themselves to perceive crafts from time to time, the vast majority of people on your world cannot deal with this or else they would see us, for we are here.

We would suggest that you enter into a negotiation with your unconscious levels. Request that they allow the barriers to come down under certain conditions, with the understanding that they will be replaced to support you in your everyday life for as long as you feel you need them. This might allow you to experience a sighting, assured that you will return to your everyday perceptions.

Allowing contact to be perceived by the conscious mind requires personal exploration of a path that would permit a nonthreatening interaction to take place. At the same time you must work to free your consciousness from the patterns of self-protective fear that act as a natural defense. This is a process and we will not project how long any individual or your world as a whole will take to accomplish this, for, as we have said, you constantly surprise us.

We can assure you of one thing: You will enter into open communication with extraterrestrial worlds. You will be part of the intergalactic community. You are just about to launch the ship of Earth on the intergalactic seas, and we wish you bon voyage!

TWENTY-SEVEN

Cliffhangers

The Pleiadian Voices and the Pleiadian Light*

In September 1994, responding to a request for information about ETs interacting openly with us, I channeled that the probable site for the initial open contact would be England. The time frame would depend on the world situation.

Since then I have asked several times for updates. What I have found more interesting than any prophecy is the picture of how probabilities shift as our world consciousness makes new choices in the creation of world events.

I am including excerpts from these channelings to show the complex issues involved in establishing open communication with our neighbors in space.

September 28, 1994. The contact event that will first catch the attention of the news media and open the floodgates for interworld communications will, at the time of this reading, not be in the United States. At this reading, for various reasons, the most likely media-oriented touchdown will be England. This will be an intergalactic operation that incorporates delegates from different ET groups.

The reasons for the choice of England are many: the language of English is widely spread on your world and could be considered your language of diplomacy. Also, the people in England have for eons been living in an energy vortex that has supported transcendent experiences. Those who have chosen to live there have been entrained to these energies.

---

* The Pleiadian Voices are our counterpart in the next dimension. The Pleiadian Light beings are now ascended entities who originated as Pleiadian Voices.

In addition, this area has been undergoing a period of preparation by being the major world site for crop-circle activity. These circles have left energy residues and provoked a lot of interest and dialogue that are also clearing the path for contact.

Another consideration is that England is on an island. This has been an ideal situation in the past, protection being provided by the surrounding sea. For our purposes this will serve to contain the event, in terms of mass public reaction, yet remain a part of the global information network.

Something else we would like to add is that the Camelot energy will be reactivated as a result of this contact. Now, this is a mythic energy dynamic that transcends the Arthurian legend and its characters. It is more like the coming of a second Round Table to establish new ideals for a new age of intergalactic interaction. This time the table will not be splintered by deception and dissension. The new Round Table will allow the Earth to sit as an equal with its celestial neighbors.

March 24, 1995. With regard to updating the material on the contact scenario, we would project that the England touchdown is still the highest probability. However, there are repeated shiftings of the time frame. There is currently a new level of chaos on your world. It is the result of the breaking down of old patterns in order to form the structure of the new world of light. Each chaotic burst resolves itself along the lines of the new patterns. This is like watching a ship battling huge waves whipped up by storms. It is hard to accurately predict the ship's course.

We can only watch these patterns. We will be there when the elements come together that blend a calming of the erratic patterns with a good level of integration of the mass consciousness and an openness to welcoming ET interaction into your world culture. Understand that we cannot allow a media-oriented event if there is a danger of shocking the world consciousness. To those who are working so enthusiastically to open contact, consider seriously what it means to enter the intergalactic consciousness: the world as you know it will never be the same. This is a sobering thought and is the reason we are very careful in our preparations.

We hope this gives you some idea of the elements and forces involved in creating this event. Perhaps this will help you to understand why we cannot give you a date, time and place. We can only present our perception of the patterns as viewed at the instant of this transmission.

We are not trying to withhold anything or mislead you; we simply do not operate in a world of absolutes. Such a world is an illusion of your plane, which can only view things at the present time in a linear progression.

We have given some clues that will help you prepare. More than that we cannot say for certain. Understand that at this time on your planet there is much more activity in terms of shifts in probable realities than you have had at more stable times in your past. These are like mutations in the time flow. This includes shifts for individuals and events as well as the flow of history.

The most important thing each of you can do is work to understand your own reality better. Then you will better understand our position in dealing with you and can be of more assistance to us. Above all, be at peace.

May 30, 1995. Regarding the contact scenario: the information we can give *at the present* is that the areas in England are still being prepared energetically for the probable touchdown. There has been a shift in energy to favor the more remote area near the Scottish border. This is because of the increase in world discord. The feeling is that the event would be better contained and kept to a lower level of impact, initially limiting the range of the release of information.

A shift in the world consciousness to purge negative energy more quickly and dramatically has caused the new level of destructive events. The mass consciousness is now playing with the idea of disaster versus disease. Choices are being made between a predominance of violent upheavals, both natural and man-made, whether disease would take a minor role in the transformation process — or the opposite, with disease used as the primary means of releasing negativity.

We must watch these considerations carefully, for they impact on how and when we can make open contact. The "where" is still England as the highest probability at the time of this reading. Trust that when you are ready to receive us and accept us, we will be there.

November 18, 1995. As an update to the media-oriented touchdown, we can tell you that the ET landing group is currently in negotiation with some leaders of your hidden government. These are not the leaders whose identities you know. They are the ones who operate behind the scenes to influence world affairs to unfold as they wish. We do not say this to frighten you, for there have always been powers behind the throne. *They do not operate without the support of the mass unconscious.*

These negotiations implemented the surfacing of the alien autopsy films. These are not artifacts that were collecting dust in the attic of a "little old man from Pasadena" or any such tale. They didn't just happen to be discovered at this fateful time.

These Earth leaders are frightened of the media. It is one area that they have not been able to truly control. Communications is a field that still welcomes mavericks and idealists (if they can pull in readers or viewers). The media is expanding and becoming more complex, even allowing open cable channels for ordinary citizens to have their voices heard. It carries the potential for the survival of individual rights during the chaos of the Earth transformation to a planet of light.

The reason the leaders fear the media is because they believe it will get out of control and cause chaos. Therefore they have agreed on a progression of revelations regarding the existence of ETs that had been hidden by former, long-dead political leaders. As the film vaults are opened, you might be surprised what comes to light.

The agenda for the touchdown at the time of this reading still has England as the highest probable site for reasons previously stated. The other aspects remain substantially the same. The time is the element in question.

We will not allow the leaders to control the media coverage of our landing, but we will negotiate with them as to the time. We feel that it will be helpful to us if they feel confident that the people have been sufficiently prepared. You might help by spreading the word that we come in peace. The groups from the

Pleiades usually open communications with this reminder, that we come in peace and joy.

April 2, 1996. Touchdown update? Do we need to tell you what has been happening in the British Isles recently? Resumed bombing by the IRA when peace was so near; the massacre of bright, shining children in Scotland; and the worldwide ban on British beef as a result of the animal kingdom giving expression to the world's insanity.

Your intuitive perceptions will tell you that open contact could not occur in this chaos. The disturbances in this particular area are signals to us that the world consciousness is definitely not ready for intergalactic interaction. There is still too much work you must do on your own world before you can handle interaction with other worlds.

It also tells us that, at least at the present, you are choosing the more rapid purging of negativity by violence dominating the slower, less aggressive purging by disease. We honor your choices.

We are aware of those who are diligently working to establish pathways for contact. We wish to emphasize that we are now making and will continue to make various forms of limited contact with individuals and small groups.

We can only say, as we have before, that the most important assistance you can give us is for each individual to work on his own integration, his own expansion of consciousness. This is how you truly reach us — not with your spaceships, but with your minds.

Be assured that we are watching for the right time for open contact and that we are assisting you with your evolution. We hear when you ask for guidance. And we will meet face to face one day. Until then, be at peace.

TWENTY-EIGHT

Contact Plan Proposed

The Pleiadian Light

This is a request for an update on the contact scenario first predicted in 1994. At that time the highest probability for a media-oriented contact was that it would be in England for reasons of language preparation, quality of energy, media center and so on.

We greet you in peace and joy. We, along with the unified ET organization (the Integrated Intergalactic Network), have been observing and documenting the Earth responses to the increase in ET/UFO material (whether true or false, conscientious, sensational, fictional or documentary) that is flooding your world media.

We do not have great expertise in opening contact with such a variegated world as yours. Your world is both a unique experiment and a natural evolutionary world like many others. Our observations are causing us to reevaluate some of the previously released information on the agenda for opening media-level contact. Understand that the contact scenario continues with many individuals and small groups on a regular basis.

In our previous experiences in opening contact with a world culture that is exploring separation and illusion and has little sense of any reality beyond its own, we have pinpointed a power center that meets the criteria needed to reach the entire world population quickly and clearly so that the information is not distorted by the resident world consciousness.

In our evaluation of the Earth world situation we chose England, for the many reasons previously stated. As we are viewing your world at this moment [April 7, 1997], we are viewing a level of world activity that is increasing in intensity but that we had projected would be decreasing in intensity by this time.

Your variegated nature includes diverse boundaries of nations, races, philosophies, economies, educational levels and so forth. You are the least homogeneous world culture with which we have ever dealt. This diversity is expanding at the present time and people all over your world are on the move, whether by desire or by force. From our perspective we see this as world chaos on many levels.

We would like to penetrate this chaos for two reasons. One, our presence on your world as a conscious reality would (after the initial intensification of chaos) serve to impel your world to blend into a unified Earth consciousness. Two, because our *open* interaction, occurring by the end of the century, would brand the new millennium as an age of exciting intergalactic exchange and a growth period for all involved.

We are considering at this time of communication (remember, this is an *update*) that England is still a valuable and important contact site. However, we are also considering that simultaneous contact events in several different power points would better serve your diverse world culture.

Please do not cast this in concrete. The following additional sites could experience simultaneous contact events that could be recorded one way or another. On the European continent, Belgium has the highest probability. In Africa, the western part of Egypt would be the chosen site. In South America, a site east of Lima, Peru. In the U.S.A., the present highest possibility would be in Arizona above the desert line. To align the Oriental energy, there is a probable site between Hong Kong and Canton. In addition, there could be simultaneous sightings of craft over Tokyo, New York and Sydney.

Please understand that we are projecting probabilities. Some, all or maybe more sites could be included. What we wish to communicate to those among you who are absorbing and holding on your plane the energies that support open contact, is that there is now a shift in the agenda, and a number of simultaneous landings and contacts hold the highest probable energy now.

Please be at peace. The peace path is an open road for us.

TWENTY-NINE

Planning for Probable Contact

The Pleiadian Light

We greet you in peace and joy. We project our energy to and through a craft on which members of the Pleiadian Voices are currently [May 4, 1997] participating in a reconnoitering mission. The mission is under the auspices of the Integrated Intergalactic Network (other channels translate other names for this organization) and involves several different ET cultures working together. The craft is within your Earth atmosphere. It is positioned above your globe over the Atlantic Ocean and is transmitting our message from there.

This organization is to reconnoiter sites that hold the highest compatible energy for a landing that would support our multi-ET away team and in which there are sufficient lightworkers who are prepared to participate in a contact event. At this reading there are sufficient contact lightworkers on Earth to be able to participate in a series of simultaneous touchdown events.

There is a period ahead in which your Northern Hemisphere experiences its season of maximum light [summer]. Traditionally you use summer to take time off from your usual endeavors, to rest and regroup. That you do this by running around your globe is sometimes lost on us, but we understand your need to break patterns and that sometimes a relief from walking (or plodding) is to run.

We are reconnoitering the possibilities that the time of shifting populations of lightworkers from one place to visit other places could provide an opportunity for positioning the "right" people in the best touchdown sites for some simultaneous contact events. We ask you, as we always do, to approach this idea in a circumspect way, understanding that we might try out many different scenarios before the time and circumstances "click" and Earth is in an open-contact mode with its intergalactic neighbors.

However, as you are planning tours and vacations this light season, if you feel impulses to go places you hadn't considered or suddenly receive money to go on an expensive sacred-sites tour or are guided in some other way to plan an unusual vacation, we suggest that you follow these impulses. It might simply prove to be a rehearsal, but things might also click. We don't know any more than you do. We simply make ourselves available for probable events to unfold and we ask that you do the same.

Because of the broad range on your world of education, cultures both insular and expansive, language and/or intuitive skills and so forth, we have a continuing concern regarding the effects of interworld contact on the deep psyche of many strata of your populations. Open contact with other worlds poses a real threat to the substructure of the psyche that holds your perceptions of world reality together. Taking in and processing a major shift in perspective also poses a threat to your religions, science and self-concepts as a world consciousness and as individuals. You can imagine your physical body suddenly being knocked off balance so violently that you fall to the ground. You would be shocked and disoriented until you recovered your feet and your balance. Imagine this happening to a world population; this is the concern we hold.

Our request is to those of you who have a grasp of what is involved in ET contact. We ask that you suggest to yourselves that you meet on the dream plane and act as ambassadors of calm, spreading reassurance among your Earth kin at this level, which is removed from waking restrictions and closer to your true spirit selves.

You have no idea, at the level at which you are reading this, how powerful such an endeavor would be. If enough work was done on the dream plane, we could land with ease in the United Nations parking lot and everyone would say, "Well, you finally got here. What took you so long?"

THIRTY

Inner/Outer Earth Connections

Maril and Hoetoefil,
Inner Earth Individuals

We are making contact [May 6, 1997] in order to establish a pattern that will include our energy and support for you in opening contact with extraterrestrials.

Maril and I, Hoetoefil, are the titular leaders of the Inner Earth civilization. Actually, we are part of a species-sentient culture, meaning that we are intuitively aware of each member of our inner world and operate as a consciousness unit. Therefore we do not need elected leaders. We represent our unified civilization in situations of interactions with others.

Our inner world is aware of and affected by the surface culture. However, we are not truly synchronous with your time-space continuum. We are on a parallel living line that is a few density degrees lighter than yours.

We have awareness and some interactions with you, but we will not be sharing the exact future path that has the highest probable energy for you. However, we are sharing the same mother world, so we regard you as kin.

We are physically shorter than your race. Our men are about the height of your women and our women are, in appearance, like your pubescent girls. There is a lightness about our physical appearance that has caused those among you who can jump dimensional walls in consciousness to mistake us for various fairy folk. Our eyes are fair shades and our hair coloring is a dozen shades of neutral.

Our interest in expanding our contact with surface terrans is to be of assistance in opening your interactions with extraterrestrials. We are in contact with many ET cultures, technologically and telepathically. In addition, we have ongoing face-to-face contacts with those who have bases beneath the surface. These bases are also in the sea and beneath the sea floor.

The ETs present on these bases have the capacity to shift dimensional levels as well as hold more than one level at a time. Therefore they can interact with you and with us and sometimes with both of us at once.

Since we are less alien to you in our vibratory identity patterns, we are in a good position to act as liaisons and assist in the contact drama. The reason why we are coming on stage at this point is because of the ETs' exploration of the idea of several simultaneous opening-contact events. Many of the sites that are being considered are also places that are large, energy-packed centers in our dimensional reality of Earth. Though we are slightly off alignment with your world, we can still provide grounding energy for the ETs and a comfortable environment for your welcoming parties at the sites aligned with power centers in our world.

Our species is a derivative of the surface Earth humans. We are one of the successful hybrid combinations that have been engineered, from time out of time, between Earth and Zeta genetics. When those of you who are familiar with the Essassani culture interact with us, you will feel that our energy is very similar. We are a manifestation of the hybrid project in a parallel reality. The Essassani are a future manifestation. They are a full-density step "higher" than you. We are about one-half step in tonal/vibrational progression from you.

Our hybrid project included keeping us within the Earth energy matrix with the hope that this mother support would enhance our chances for surviving and enduring. This has proven to be valuable and successful in the creation of our genetic species.

Like the Essassani, we are bound in a cultural unit by telepathy and species awareness. However, we retain the use of speech and written language. In many characteristics, we are closer to you.

Many of you feel the Zeta/Earth-hybrid project was entirely for the benefit of the poor, "cloned-out" Zetas. This feeds the resentment of many who remember participating in the hybrid projects and feel terrorized and violated. The procedures translate this way in your present perceptions, and the project directors understand this to one degree or another.

Imagine yourself as a medieval farmer whose only experience with the pattern of illness/healing is with herbal remedies passed down through family tradition. View how such a person would react to a day of tests in one of your ordinary hospitals: needles being stuck into him, blood being taken, examining doctors probing him and huge machines doing God knows what. Many of the participants in the hybrid projects have been exposed to similar situations. Their terrors are understandable, but by gaining a broader view, the participants can help themselves release their victim identification.

Another helpful view of the project is to understand that the Zetas are not the only ones benefiting. There are balancing aspects that benefit the terran contributors to the project. Many of the most painful aspects of Earth life have to do with the exploration of separation. Terrans are as extreme in their individual isolation as Zetas are in their cookie-cutter sameness. Terrans are isolated one from another, individual from community, community from national groups, nationalities from world consciousness and so forth, expanding to God source. This is not something you are acutely aware of in your daily conscious life, but every aspect of your culture is encapsulated and prevented from viewing the true relatedness of all.

The isolation from God source is the most cruel form of separation because it means being cut off from home. Earth beings not only lose contact with their true home, but the limit of their five senses isolates them from each other.

The addition of Zeta genetics to terran genetics has produced humanoid groups with very close emotional and psychic ties to one another and a unified sense of community. As a result, the Earth-Zeta hybrids are basically very happy, harmonious people. This is no small gift to the terran aspect of the project. Part of the energy drive for the terran civilization has been a built-in discontent that forces beings to keep going, keep producing, keep consuming, although experiencing very little contentment and happiness.

The families of hybrids evolved from the blending of Earth and Zeta genetics have formed very successful civilizations. The Zeta genetic line has gained diversity from Earth elements and the Earth line of development has gained cohesiveness and unity from the Zetas. All are dimensionally progressed from the present 3D Earth.

There is a sensing among those of you who can intuit expanded realities that the "terrorizing abductions" have been suspended or called off. This is only one probable line and not the line from which we dictate this material. On our line of reality the projects continue. Those to whom we address this have shifted to a new probable line of progress. On this probable line there is an understanding in the deep psyche of the creativity and intrinsic benevolence of the project. When you shift, all your perceptions shift. Much of the terror has been lifted and has been replaced by an inner knowing of the benign nature of the plan.

We feel that you have been expanding with great speed in the levels of reality you are able to accommodate. Because of this we are going to push your perceptions a little further. Our Inner Earth species is not the only such group of beings; however, the other species are occupying different bands of alternate reality. We feel as though our civilization is the only Inner Earth one, just as you perceive yourselves to be the human Earth species. However, we both have many parallel versions of ourselves.

We have more ability to access these alternate selves than you do at the present time. We also have much greater facility in awareness and ability to contact you than you have to contact us. By interacting with you, we hope to communicate that there is a rich world of multidimensional realities surrounding you. As we open contact with more and more of you, the sense of isolation you carry, like a given whose pain is not even recognized, will begin to recede. This emptiness will be filled with an awareness of the rich vibrational world that links you with All That Is.

Our intention in presenting these thoughts and information about our/your Earth is to help you open to extraterrestrials who are moving to open contact between our and their worlds. We are terrans, too. We are your cousins. The intergalactic travelers are also cousins. You come from a big family!

THIRTY-ONE

A Pleiadian Energy Theater

Spandia

This is Spandia. I am a Pleiadian female and a future incarnation of this channel living in a time about 400 years in your future. In my world culture I am a creative artist. My work is in a form of theater not unlike yours, in that it allows us to expand our own experience of dimensions by vicariously participating in the dramas presented to us. However, the theater work I do does not use live actors. I am a "thought artist" and my theater is created entirely by my mind and imagination projected as energy that forms images for others to view.

I work in a circular theater with a domed ceiling similar to a planetarium. The audience sits around the circumference of the building while the artist projecting the presentation sits in the center. The surface of the dome and walls above the heads of the audience are sensitized to allow thought energy created by the artist to form images on it. The sensitized surface is calibrated to pick up only the performing artist's thoughts and no random thoughts from the audience. Projecting thoughts onto this surface requires some discipline on the part of the artist in maintaining the correct "frequency" for transmission.

The images play all around the audience and involve productions that would be called total theater on your world — video developed to a maximum. This includes music and abstract color forms as well as representational images. There are also elements of channeling involved in thought theater. Dramas unfold. Movement flows that would be considered dance. Sounds are heard that could be vocal, instrumental or from sources that transcend physically created sonic production. All this and more is part of our theater.

My interactions with this channel [Hannah Beaconsfield] have allowed me to garner Earth dramas to present for my home audience. These dramas not only expand our experiences but help us understand you, our cousins, as we prepare to enter into open contact with your world.

There is another form of thought theater in which I participate. It is the creation of holographic images. In this activity there are usually three artists working together. We sit in a triangular formation and blend our energies to create images in the center where our energies converge. Often this work results in a sculptural piece that we each help to refine. It can also be a drama where characters act out a scenario. We usually confer before the performance on a general outline. Then we allow the characters to take off on their own.

These theatrical skills can be developed on your world as well. There are already individuals with natural abilities to affect sensitive surfaces such as film, video or audio tape with energy from their minds or hands. They do not yet have refined skills, but that can be developed. This is a future path for the arts on your world as well.

The holographic theater is a game you can play right now. With two or more participants you can create your own energy theater. The more closely aligned the participants are, the more successful you are likely to be. Many Earth beings have pronounced abilities to project energy, as in healing with the hands. Even those without pronounced abilities can template the abilities of others by working closely with the able ones, then contribute to such projects.

I would suggest that three participants sitting in a triangular arrangement would be best to create this holographic imaging. Enter into a meditative state and allow the energy to flow as you project it from your brow chakra, your eyes or your hands to a point in the center of the triangle where your energies meet. Picture yourself as a conduit for the energy so you are not depleting your own energy stores. I would suggest you start by creating simple shapes in space: spheres, cubes or pyramids.

At first use your hands to feel the shapes, working to give greater "solidity" to what you feel. You can then move on to energy forms that can be seen. Simply start by forming an area of light. Red light is often easiest to begin with. Then work on expanding the light and changing the color.

Variations of this game are being played by many on the Earth plane even now. I would like to suggest a dimension that you could include. If one or more of your participants is a channel, you can call in extraterrestrial energy to play with you. Conceivably, you could work together to form images of the extraterrestrial's reality. The Earth participants would provide the life-force energy and the extraterrestrials could manipulate that energy to create images from their worlds. Those games could even be recorded on tape or film.

The degree of success of such a venture would depend on how well the individuals blend their abilities. Like other collaborative creative combinations on your plane, such as composers and lyricists or actors and playwrights, a really great team can produce wonderful creations.

These games are fun and have practical applications, too. They assist in the expansion process of the consciousness of your plane as you move into the age of light. Also, when you call in extraterrestrial participation, you are supporting the preparation for open contact with other worlds.

THIRTY-TWO

Crop Circles

The Pleiadian Light

Crop-circle designs have been placed on your Earth surface as images of communication from otherworld cultures. The extraterrestrials whose collaborative creation of these proportionately huge markings on the Earth are tripping deep memories for you of having seen these symbols in other times, places and dimensions. These images are bypassing your intellect and reaching your deep psyche with a greeting that is recognized at that level.

Another element of this form of artistic expression is that it is intended to be viewed from the air. In intergalactic communities where space travel is common, this form of expression is often seen. These images also act as signposts or points of recognition. This type of creative expression was practiced on Earth in your ancient past and presently by Earth artists.

The overriding reason extraterrestrials are contributing these markings to your world now [February 1994] is not so much to communicate some complex message, but to prepare you for entry into the intergalactic community. These geometric shapes trigger deep intuitive feelings of having seen these images somewhere before, and there is an element of comfort in this.

Crop Circles Update

White Crow

The new harvest of crop circles [July 1996] represents more

refined and complex communications than some of the earlier ones. They are an exciting indication of the progress in interaction between the ET groups and the mass consciousness of this planet.

The earlier markings were ET creations to get your attention. When the markings had the attention of your conscious perceptions, a cocreated project began in which you shared in the input. These images are intended to communicate messages through sacred geometry or geometric chords, not translate to verbal messages directed to the intellect. These images are intended to be perceived by your conscious minds in the way you view art. That is, they create a feeling when viewing them: delight, awe or admiration for the beauty and design.

Riding this feeling, the geometric message is carried into the deep psyche, which accommodates reality on its most basic level. This includes the shape, form and relationship of geometric figures. These elemental symbols define your reality.

Different intergalactic species can be represented by different combinations of basic geometric shapes. You can communicate with each other the distinctions of your world realities by translating them into geometric forms.

This is a simplified explanation. Remember that crop circles are multidimensional symbols. We are simply giving you another dimension to consider. There are other symbolic aspects included in some of the different figures, such as sonics, mathematical equations and celestial configurations.

You might try creating your own images to get a firsthand feeling for the process.

THIRTY-THREE

Follow-up on the England Expedition

The Pleiadian Light

This channeling was requested by Barbara Angelakis for participants of a tour of England arranged by Transformative Journeys into the Light. This tour was led by Lyssa Royal-Holt and Shari Adamiak of CSETI.

The England expedition was an overwhelming success. Your energies literally blasted open a hole in the consciousness shield that encapsulates your third-density world psyche.

At the same time, with the exquisite synchronicity of spirits working in perfect harmony, the film *Independence Day* was opening all across the United States. The response to this movie was so great that it established new box-office records. Even if you weren't one of the millions who saw it, you were still inundated with news stories, interviews and the mass hoopla that this film generated. And what was this film about? — aliens invading and destroying your world.

While you were generating energy to blast open a hole in the third-dimensional psyche, there was a huge number of Earth individuals who were releasing deep-seated fears concerning alien contact. These are fears that must be given expression in order to clear the way emotionally for contact to take place on a mass level.

So many times what you judge as painful, frightening and/or negative is simply energy being used by more expanded levels of yourselves in very creative ways. Do note that the film was not named *Alien Cannibals* or *Intergalactic Road Warriors*, but *Independence Day*. You are freeing yourselves from the emotional baggage that hampers forward movement on several different frontiers.

And the drama continues: The announcement of life on Mars by reputable NASA scientists was the next act in an accelerating scenario. This announcement itself is more important than any explanations that we can give regarding life on Mars. Of course, Mars has entertained life for eons: indigenous life at both surface and inner Mars, intergalactic colonists and way stations, Earth outposts and so forth.

Right now, following the success on many levels of *Independence Day*, this announcement is part of the preparation for contact that is accelerating. The information has been available for release for some time. It came out now with a little help from the covert powers that are orchestrating things. As a matter of fact, the hidden powers are being pushed to the wall because with or without their agreement, the mass consciousness is demanding that the doors open for ET contact. Your group was actively contributing to this major drama during your trip.

In fact, the mass consciousness is becoming more cohesive and will become more powerful than the covert powers, for all they have is money. The energy generated by a cohesive mass consciousness is a much more powerful energy than the energy of money.

The welcoming crop circles that you are exploring were formed before and during your visit as a part of this whole mass event. The recording and disseminating of these images — though not on the level of a blockbuster movie — is moving them through the mass consciousness by being passed from one person to another among those who have particular interest in this phenomenon.

These images, designated the Helix and the Snail, are very complex cocreated energy/form information units. The translation of these on the full range of their multiple levels would create a library of written material. Fortunately, this material is not intended to be absorbed in that manner, though some key points can be converted into intellectually understood information for total integrative purposes. The mass of information is intended to be intuitively grasped by those who view the images. This was the ETs' contribution to the blockbuster week of preparation for contact.

The glyphs are created by an ET technology using a vibrational energy that on Earth translates into sonic patterning, though beyond the range of Earth-human hearing. However, some animals and humans in a heightened or altered state can register such an auditory signal.

There are craft equipped to create this phenomenon, much like your skywriting planes. These craft operate under the banner of the united intergalactic organization that is like your United Nations. In the simplest terms, they create a computer image that becomes a stencil for the glyph. The location is entered into the computer and the image is stamped sonically on the surface vegetation. The effect is like a gentle, whirling breeze that swirls the stalks into a clear-cut pattern, bending them without breaking. The whole glyph is usually created in one burst of sonic energy.

The Snail glyph was, as Sasha (channeled by Lyssa Royal-Holt) correctly noted, a cocreated pattern in which the tour group participated. On the dream plane, you were out of your bodies and riding in the glyph-maker craft. Your joint effort didn't have quite the same cohesive aesthetic level as the "professional" designers, but you had a lot of fun doing it.

Your visit to Avebury was for the purpose of reactivation. This site has been a welcoming place for craft landings from the time it was still part of Atlantis, and it might be so again. The Avebury energy is a powerful vortex where dimensional membranes are very thin and where outer- and inner-Earth energies often break through barriers and meet.

The entire British Isles — it was a single land mass for a while after the fall of Atlantis — has always been a portal for Inner Earth energies. There have been times in history when the right elements converged and the doorways on either side of the dimensional barrier became aligned. For brief periods outer- and inner-Earth realities mingled. Some of the tales believed to be about the devic kingdom were either about or influenced by these interactions.

Avebury was also the site for massive ceremonial events. During the post-Atlantean period, before civilization revisited more primitive expressions and when memories of the Atlantean culture were still strong, this power place in England was a seasonal ceremonial meeting ground. Many came from all the lands nearby where Atlantean refugees had settled, even from Mediterranean shores. They came in a great regatta of boats to this sacred place, the last fragment of the Atlantean continent.

As civilization went into a decline, the Avebury ceremonial grounds became a center for sects that employed human sacrifice in the hope of generating energies that would regain for them their former power and glory. In the progression of history many groups used this sacred place, sensing its power. All have left energetic residues of their sojourn.

We are going to go out on a probable limb right now [August 12, 1996]. (Please do not get carried away with this idea and dismiss other probabilities that might later be a better summation of the energy patterns.) We will say there has been a reawakening of ancient energies in the Avebury circle, and it could serve as a sacred meeting place once more for intergalactic contact.

In any case, our congratulations to all of you who participated in the total drama of this one further step toward intergalactic unity. Our peace is your peace.

What information can you give regarding Stonehenge and the powerful energy felt at its center point?

The center point of the Stonehenge circle, with its quaking vibration, is a coordination point on the circumterra grid, aligned with an Inner Earth vortex and potentiated with energy reflected and redirected by the great stones. The stones act as mirrors to intensify the energy (as a mirror intensifies and directs sunlight to start a fire). When the stones had a full complement of lintels, they also acted to ground the energy. In addition, the stones were arranged to align with natural Earth forces such as polar directions and seasonal energies.

This energy used a conductor in the form of a human priest or priestess (determined by the season in which the energy was being generated) to complete the circuitry. Those who acted as conductors for this energy trained intensively to handle the power. Through their conductivity they made the energy available to all participants in much the same way that electricity is conducted by touch until it is grounded.

The original purpose for the energy/structure that is Stonehenge was for travel in time, space and dimensions. This energy source was able to merge physical matter and consciousness — that is, convert physical matter into consciousness units — for the purpose of freely accessing other dimensions. This is a bit more complicated than astral projection.

Your scientist Tesla had memories of using energy in this way and tried to replicate it with the available technology. He became accustomed to handling high voltages of energy. A modern-day foray (in which Tesla participated) into using energy in this manner was attempted in the project you know as the Philadelphia Experiment. The missing element that would have made Tesla's projects more successful is the nature of the human participants who were used. These projects require humanoid versions with much less density and a far greater expansion of consciousness.

The culture that created this energy center precedes anything within your historical concepts, and its source was extraterrestrial. They were a colony of Sirian consciousness units that took up quasi-humanoid form and worked on the creation of some of the animal species. This translates as an artistic group project. They had no need to work with a highly developed mechanical technology, for their command of consciousness/energy technology served all their needs.

The original Stonehenge was not the physical edifice you see today, but an energetic model for the present structure. If you were there at the time and had auric vision, you would have seen a light structure in shimmering colors closely resembling the current image. However, this light structure indelibly stamped the site with the "power center" energy that inspired later civilizations to create the stone arrangement you now see.

In the evolution of the history of the Stonehenge site, those who followed used the power center for their own purposes. When some of the original Sirian colonists elected to move into denser forms and establish a lineage on Earth, they began to lose the skills in handling the energy.

There was a time when the use of death energy, of human sacrifice, could provide the necessary conductivity to activate various consciousness permutations. Then that potential was lost, too. However, the power of the original energy/edifice construction was so strong that it maintained the structure and its power in a latent state for untold centuries.

Part 4

Finale

THIRTY-FOUR

Perfecting Integration

Come Down to Where You Ought to Be

Grace

There is a definite pattern to the placement of lightworkers on your world. On prebirth and spirit levels individuals have chosen the territories in which they find themselves. The placement is determined by familiarity with the energy terrain, the proximity of soul-family members for support and the location where the individual's talents and skills can be put to the best use.

At the present time the strategic placement of lightworkers in an evenly dispersed pattern is serving to hold the light energy on this plane. As the situation shifts and some areas require more tethering than others, you will see people suddenly getting an impulse to move to a new area. This is already happening. It will, in all probability, continue until the new light energy is stabilized on your world.

Within this strategic placement there is another pattern forming. Lightworkers who are vibrationally aligned and/or have spiritual agreements to work together and support each other are convening to form light bases. These bases can have a variety of forms, from communelike groups to very loose communities or electronically connected worldwide networks.

No matter where the individuals are located, they have subjective experiences that are very similar and can be sufficiently agreed upon to enable them to provide comfort and support for each other. The changes, due to the increase in light energy and the clearing of the bodies of consciousness, are similar enough that you can agree that something is definitely happening. These are expressed as physical and emotional symptoms.

Another aspect that is considered in an individual's placement is the past-life experiences in that location that have left an energy residue. This provides a sense of familiarity with the area, language, culture and a feeling of being at home.

Remember, however, that on the dream plane you are all in touch with one another and have a clear picture of the shifting characteristics of the mass consciousness of Earth. If you suggest to yourselves in your waking state that you become more aware of your dream-plane interactions and negotiations, you will feel more at peace in your particular territory.

Making a Meadow

Your world is poised at the point of maximum separation from the center of all energy, or the Source. The pendulum is now beginning its sweep back to Source. The dichotomy of opposites on your world is so pervasive as to make it almost impossible to imagine what sort of reality would evolve from the integration of these polarities. Very little vocabulary is available with which we can convey the nature of integration.

You have questioned us: "Certainly, there is right and wrong, evil and goodness, isn't there? What will happen when we integrate our gender energies? Will the spark that occurs between positive and negative charges go out of our relationships? What will we have as a civilization when we integrate the horror and brutality of some nations with the idealism and freedom of others? Will we be mixing dirt with water and end up with mud?"

We understand your inability to grasp a reality that you don't even have words to define. We often use analogies or stories, for they are like dream dramas and can contain much more in symbolic content than can be conveyed by words. By way of explanation we will simply say that the reality you will experience when negative and positive are integrated will veer toward what you would currently define as positive.

As an analogy, we will present you with a dream drama that will grow in your consciousness: You have two lots of land adjoining each other. One is a beautifully manicured flower garden. Next to it is a vacant lot with weeds, broken tree branches, mud puddles and trash. You take down the fence between the lots and go away for several years, allowing the natural elements to take over. When you return to the spot your eyes light up and you say, "What a beautiful meadow!" All the elements of both lots have integrated and the result is a reality that you would define by the positive term "meadow."

THIRTY-FIVE

Probable Future Economic Systems

The Pleiadian Light

Many ET cultures at levels more developed than the Earth culture have economic systems that are variations of an equal-value system. We will present our version of the system and a perspective on its ideal unfolding. We will call it the *economics of ecstasy*.

Let us give you an overview. The system, in brief, is a nonmonetary form of exchange. However, it is not a barter system, for in such a system there is still an assigning of relative values to different endeavors and different products. The economics of the ecstasy system is based on the awareness of the truth that all individuals are equal parts of the consciousness of the God source. Therefore, anything they do or produce is equal to anything anyone else does or makes. Each individual does whatever delights him/her most and makes it freely available to others. This way everyone has available whatever they want. Because it is in the natural flow of things, it all balances perfectly. The ETs, contrary to what you might think, do not end up with a civilization of baseball players and ballerinas.

This system necessitates a society that has evolved sufficiently to be able to truly pursue its own happiness. It is dependent on being free from competitive forces, concepts of limitation and the belief in a scale of value. This system flows in a natural exchange and operates in most humanoid cultures that have evolved to the dimension that is the next step for you.

There are some variations and different levels of development from one world culture to another, but this is the type of economic system you are moving toward. How and when you go about making the change is up to you. You will map out your own game plan for this and all the other changes that will occur as you move into the age of light. You might break down your present system in a dramatic restructuring, or you might evolve slowly in comfort.

The way you can work toward this ideal is the same as in any other area of this major transformation: Work on yourself first. As more and more people open themselves to the understanding of their true equality and allow self-love to support their endeavors, you will be able to move toward this form of economy. As the grains of sand accumulate, eventually one grain will shift the scales. Then it will seem like this has always been the way, and you won't be able to imagine how you tolerated past systems.

On your world money equals power. Only when each of you reclaim your own power will you make it impossible for others to garner power through wealth.

Individuals in your world are presently programmed to fit into a system geared to benefit the most powerful organizations rather than the individual. Various types of pressure are brought upon you to keep you in the established pattern; most of these pressures are based on fear, not reward.

However, in the last twenty-five or thirty years of your culture, many individuals have moved out of the mainstream to free themselves from the struggle, strife and stress. Some have felt the pain of being ridiculed and ostracized; however, they are the trailblazers. They are holding open the door of the dream that every individual can have an autonomous life doing what he loves to do best.

Within the security of your present situation you can begin to shift to this new reality simply by allowing yourself to do what you really want to do most in any situation where it is possible. This involves listening carefully to your true desires and isolating them from the beliefs about what you "should" be doing or what someone else wants you to do.

You might be surprised how little you do for your own joy. As you begin this in small ways, you are joining your energy to a movement that will evolve into the ideal economic structure we call the economics of ecstasy.

THIRTY-SIX

Assisting Life-End Transitions

Grace

The new age of light that you are entering presents a great deal of chaos and stress as you break old patterns to form a new world consciousness. There are many spirits who wish to be present to experience this dynamic time. So you have what you consider to be an over population problem.

There are also many spirit energies who are not excited by the prospect of this transition. They are choosing to leave Earth and return at a future point when more serene conditions prevail. We wish to give some information to those who are staying for the fireworks but who see many of their companions choosing to depart.

Many in your Western world culture do not have a strong sense of a life after death. Often those who are on the brink of transitioning are also divided against themselves. The spirit has a wider perspective on why death has been chosen, but the fearful part refuses to give up and fights with great ferocity to remain alive. Others are reluctant to leave because they fear losing contact with loved ones or because they have responsibilities they feel they can't leave. Whatever causes individuals to resist transition, that resistance can cause pain and suffering, preventing a peaceful death.

A peaceful crossing-over affords the spirit a joyful reentry onto the nonphysical plane and supports its progress on the next levels of their growth and exploration. It is recognized that an easy, trauma-free birth on this world gives an infant a good start in life. The same is true in the birthing to the next plane. Whatever the situation, if you are present at the terminal point for a person, you can be of energetic assistance. The assistance you can give is to help create an aperture through which the spirit can leave.

When an infant is born, its skull is not completely closed because in the first few months the spirit comes and goes from the body frequently as it reacclimates to Earth life. The physical aperture in the skull facilitates this. When someone has lived an Earth life and is ready to leave (and, in all good humor, has become "hard-headed"), you can assist his transition by opening an energy aperture.

If you have time alone with the person or are with others who support and understand what you are doing, you can undertake the following procedure.

> *Call in the white light to surround you and the one transitioning. Ask that spirit guides and angelic beings who are connected to the departing spirit, surround the spirit and support his/her crossing over.*
>
> *Place your left hand on the crown chakra of the one who is departing. Visualize this center opening. Move your hand slowly away from the crown, visualizing a column of magnetic energy leading out of the crown chakra. This creates an energy passage through which the spirit can exit.*
>
> *Next, place the first two fingers of your right hand on the brow chakra. This will close off the third eye. Tell the departing spirit that the door is open and they are free to leave whenever they are ready. Ask them to go in peace and leave the rest to the guides and angelic beings.*

It is interesting that the last rites of some of your present religious practices still carry elements of this energetic procedure, which was known in ancient times.

This assistance can be done from a distance just as easily, for your thoughts and intentions transcend time and space. You could also suggest to yourself before you go to sleep that you will make contact and give assistance on the dream plane to the one about to transition.

Remember that we are always available to support you, whether you are transitioning yourself or assisting another.

THIRTY-SEVEN

Image-Makers, Dream-Makers

Spandia

All creativity on the present plane and dimension of Earth is a form of channeling. With regard to the fine arts of painting and sculpture and the commercial arts of illustration and graphic design, the differences are not of greater or lesser value (except to art dealers) but in the channeled input. This input is in the sources accessed and the ratios of contribution. In all cases the artist brings to the collaboration the skills with which he/she was born, the skills she acquired and the aspects of her total human self she is most focused on and most values. These focus/value aspects can shift throughout the life of the artist due to personal circumstances and the influence of the channeled guidance her art receives.

The image-makers serve many valuable functions for their communities. Historically they have created records of their cultures. They have given visual images to sacred concepts. They have made pictures to go with stories. And, possibly most important, they have served to create a window to the subconscious of the mass consciousness. They are the dream-makers.

An artist creates a work that presents many of the subconscious rivers of probability that surge through the national, religious, economic and cultural aspects of the artist's origin. His/her style, color sense, taste in images and traditional or iconoclastic impulses serve viewers like the elements of a dream serve the dreamer. In this case the artist is dreaming for his community. It is shortsighted to pursue an artist's biography for clues to the meaning of his art. Approach it as you approach a dream, understanding that it holds symbols that are multidimensional in meaning.

The channeled contributions to the art are defined by you as inspiration. In your ancient mythology you attributed it to the muses. These are simply ways of translating a deep inner knowing that you, the artist, are receiving help and guidance from levels you don't understand. The level of inspiration is simply the level of channeled input you receive. Input can range from a former lifetime to angelic assistance.

At different times an artist will access different levels, depending on the project. This idea can threaten an artist's ego, so we feel we must point out that the conscious use of this knowledge can improve the quality of your art.

Great art — the work you designate as genius — is very often a perfect blending of talent, acquired skill and an open consciousness capable of accessing the highest levels of channeled input. This work has the quality of transcendence. These are the works of art that live with continued vitality through your ages.

The next skill acquisition for artists is the conscious understanding and development of collaborative channeling abilities.

THIRTY-EIGHT

Dreams, the Other Half of Your Life

The Pleiadian Light

Your life on Earth is divided into waking and sleeping. The part of your life spent sleeping might not be equal in time to your waking life, but it is equal in value. This dreamtime does not exist just to serve the waking life. It is not only to rest the physical and replenish your mental reserves or even to give vent to emotions that can't be expressed on the living level. It is the other half of your life and equal in value and importance to anything accomplished in the waking state.

Understand that your physical world is a creation of mass consciousness, with its energy link to Source, for the purpose of experiencing challenges and expanding dimensions. It is like one of your theater productions. You create imaginary theatrical worlds in imitation of the creativity of God source.

In a theatrical production the waking state would be represented by the moments an actor is on stage acting in the drama. In a drama you know you are acting in a play and that when it is over you will leave the theater and return to "real life." During the run of the show of your life on Earth, there is an illusion that the play is real life and that you never leave the stage until you die — your final exit.

However, you (the actor) leave the stage every night and return to real life, which is the plane of reality on which your spirit operates outside of a physical body. This is the sleep/dream state — your nightly return to real life.

Dreams have been interpreted and studied with fascination since the humanoid species gained self-awareness. Every individual and every culture has had theories about the meaning of dreams. Some dream symbols contain the mythic level of the mass consciousness. However, much of an individual's dream material contains his/her own personal use of symbolism. No one can truly interpret the dream but the dreamer, although one skilled at dream studies can offer suggestions about interpretations and guide the dreamer to understand how to unlock his own symbols.

When you begin to work with your dreams, by encouraging yourself to remember them and put the information gained to use, the pathway for exchanging information will become wider and wider. Once you open interactions with your dreaming self, you will realize how limited your life was before the dream input.

You can expand the range of your dream language, like acquiring vocabulary, to extend what you are able to "talk" about. For example, you see a nature program on TV in which the narrator says that in many ancient cultures the turtle symbolized longevity and wisdom. Shortly after this you dream about a turtle. When you wake you realize your dreaming self has signaled that this symbol with this interpretation is being added to your data bank. There are many ways that the expansion of communication between your waking and dreaming selves can be brought about; this is just one.

Most of the information we are presenting is understood by your common sense and is available for study in your various disciplines that utilize psychology. These disciplines will also teach you that dreams are multidimensional. That is the nature of symbols; they hold many layers of information.

We would like to address another aspect of the sleep/dream state that has been given less consideration. You are, at the intrinsic level, a spirit simply operating through a body. This spirit is free to leave the body when it is asleep and might very well participate in activities that do not require a body or are not possible when operating through a body.

Some of you, as spirits out of the body, act as guides for others. Many of you are there to help spirits who have passed out of the body in death to feel welcome and adjust to their new status. There are also those among you, many of whom are walk-ins, who go home in your sleep excursions to other dimensions of reality or to ET world cultures where you have stronger attachments than to Earth.

All of you are capable of interacting with each other on this plane, solving problems, giving mutual support, making agreements to meet and interact in the future and much more. This type of activity on the sleep/dream plane does not need to create a dream message for you to remember when you wake up. This activity simply changes life situations by whatever has taken place while out of the body.

This process goes on naturally; it always has and always will. However, sleep time is an opportunity that, once recognized, can be used to assist your waking life. You can ask to meet on the sleep plane difficult people with whom you are having trouble. Ask that the understandings reached on this plane naturally and easily reflect your waking life. This applies to helping children with the challenges of growing up or meeting with pets to open lines of communication with the animal world. Almost anything can be addressed on the sleep plane, for in this state your spirit is free. You can't impose your will on others through this means, but you can meet and experience open communication.

We cannot emphasize enough how important the use of the sleep/dream plane is, particularly at this time when you are beginning your integration as a world consciousness for a return to the Source. It is an incredible untapped resource for transformation.

As you begin to blend your levels of consciousness, which is part of the whole process of polarity integration, you will find that more of the material that was formerly handled on the dream level begins appearing in waking life. This is what happens when consciousness expands; it blends layers that were formerly separated and makes them available for common conscious use.

When this happens, fewer dreams are remembered from the

sleep plane. They are not needed any longer because the conscious self has begun to recognize and receive the same information by looking around its waking life. This is a looking-glass world; you cannot perceive anything that does not reflect some aspect of self. As your dreams reflect symbolic aspects of self, so too does your waking life reflect who you are, what challenges you have taken on and where you are on your journey.

The reflecting also takes on the sense of magnetizing or drawing to you images that show powerful emotional patterns. You will magnetize or draw reflections of what you love, what you fear and what you desire. This type of reflection means to bring these energies into your sphere of existence.

We refer to specific waking incidents as "real-life dream dramas" and we interpret them exactly the same as sleep-time dreams. The unconscious portions of the self will often lead you intuitively to participate passively (or sometimes actively) in dramas your total self needs to experience. These real-life dream dramas seem to be set into your life with a kind of energetic parenthesis around them. We will give you an example.

You go into a store. While you are looking around you see a young girl talking to the clerk behind the counter, whom she seems to know. She is crying and saying she has lost her keys and can't get into her apartment. She wants to use the phone to try to reach someone who might help her. She is extremely upset and the clerk is trying to calm her. He offers her the phone and she is crying even more to the person she finally reaches. You avoid going to the counter because you don't want to intrude, and you wander around the store unobtrusively. Finally the girl calms down and you go to the counter, pay for your items and leave.

Outside you realize you are unnerved and/or irritated and wonder why you had to be an unwitting observer of this drama. You were there for a reason. The drama has some meaning for you, and if you regard it exactly like a dream, you will see why you were drawn to that time and place to be a participant.

We won't insert any interpretation of this example, for each person who might have been present would find a different message for himself in it.

Another aspect of this type of unconscious event attraction is self-observation as a life barometer. There are times of confusion when you don't know what you should do or where you should go. The spirit level has an overview that allows future events and incoming influences to be observed. Working intuitively through impulses, the spirit guides the waking consciousness to what is needed in order to be prepared for the future. In other words, if you don't know what to do, watch what you are already doing, and that will give you a clue.

For example, it is midwinter. You see a bathing suit on sale that is perfect, half the price it will be in the spring. It's what you really want, but you can't justify buying it in the middle of winter. The impulse to buy nags at you until you decide it's too good a bargain to lose. Two weeks later you are invited on a Caribbean cruise.

This is a rather broad example, but this type of intuitive interaction goes on constantly in more subtle ways between the expanded and the limited levels of the self. When you encourage yourselves to listen more carefully, the voice of your spirit will become clearer and clearer.

We reiterate how important your dreaming life is, whether asleep or awake. It is a rich world that both counterbalances and expands the elements of your consciousness. It is a source of healing, of creativity and of major changes on all levels.

When great numbers of individual spirits meet on the dream level at crisis points in the growth of civilizations, they can negotiate the change of world events. If every night each of you suggested to yourselves that you meet with all others who earnestly wish for peace on Earth no matter what side of any conflict you are on, a world-changing dream could be created. This dream could alter waking reality.

There is much more freedom on the sleep/dream plane, so it is a resource for change that transcends what can be done by simply working through the waking "real" world.

THIRTY-NINE

Cutting the Cord

The Pleiadian Light

While doing a body-balancing meditation, passing my hands above my body and channeling golden light energy, I suddenly became aware of an etheric cord attached to my physical navel. At that same moment the Pleiadian Light began downloading the following channeling in my mind's ear.

The time has come to sever the etheric cord that ties you to a specific genetic family, cultural heritage and DNA pattern. These are harmonic components of the bodies of consciousness you have inherited. This will allow you to move onto the next level of your work on this world.

You have passed through many initiations in your adjustment to operating in a gift body on Earth. As you sever this etheric attachment to the physical form, you are freeing the patterns of the spirit self to make changes and pulling in abilities on many levels that are not compatible with the original attachments.

Your creative consciousness can make changes in your physical form and expand your intellectual and intuitive capacities in ways that are restricted by former patterns. Many walk-ins have been moving beyond their time of adjustments and severing this connection automatically on unconscious or dream levels.

Now we would like to give you a conscious procedure for severing this attachment. Understand that this action is not to be undertaken until there is an intuitive sensing of the right time. This is when the caretaker is aware that the walk-in spirit has assumed the control position in the life and they both are at peace with the situation. You might then use the following meditation.

As the Pleiadian Light began to instruct me in this severing procedure, I experienced a flare of fear. They reassured me, stating that this did not mean that I would feel disconnected from friends or family who are part of my heritage in this life, and that the ability to sustain or release any relationships on the basis of emotional attachments would remain. They also said that I would not feel untethered or uprooted, which made me feel more secure as a walk-in.

They explained that the physical umbilical cord is connected to the genetic, cultural and historical heritage of the physical form and has an etheric equivalent that remains after the umbilical connecting the child to the physical mother is cut. This is not the silver cord that is the tether in astral projections and the individual's link with the universal white-light energy or God. In fact, the procedure would include strengthening this very attachment. As a result, the life circumstances would be aligned with less specific and more universal potentials for growth.

Feeling reassured, I allowed them to proceed with their instructions.

Place your right hand over your navel and your left hand on your heart center. Visualize the universal white light entering your crown chakra. This light suffuses your body, then exits through your root chakra and your feet. It takes firm root in the Earth, held securely by terran energy.

Now visualize an energy loop from your heart into your left hand and arm, then down your right arm and into your navel through your right hand.

Next, use the first two fingers of your right hand to cut, like a pair of scissors, the etheric cord of Earth family attachment. See it severed at the core of your being, not just on the surface.

Keeping your "cutting" fingers at the point of severance, place your left hand over the right, palm up. See a cord of brilliant white light magnetized to your left palm. Turn the left hand over and place it on your navel while removing the right hand. See this cord of brilliant white light securely attached at your navel, linking you to an expanded heritage more universal in the level and nature of creative energy.

I asked the Pleiadian Light if this procedure had an application that would be useful to starseeds and lightworkers. They replied:

For starseeds, a reverse type of procedure would make them feel more at home on Earth. They could consciously visualize a strengthening of their etheric cord of attachment to their Earth family's genetic heritage. They might see this cord throbbing with white-light energy and surrounded by a glow of brilliant green. Green is a color closely associated with Earth because of the verdant plant life on this world. It is also the color of the heart chakra and of unconditional love for the Earth-humanoid species.

This type of meditation can assist starseeds in feeling more comfortable and can accelerate a shift in their self-concept from alien to Earthling. The parents of a starseed can also do this meditation, giving real support to their child's adjustment on this world.

As to lightworkers, which all Earth dwellers are intrinsically, a regular meditation drawing in white-light energy to suffuse all the bodies of consciousness will maintain their clarity as conduits for the light. Each lightworker is adding his/her weight to the critical mass that will transmute this planet into a lightworld.

Once again we remind all that our energy, angelic assistance and personal guides are working with you all the time. You have a massive support system for your transformation as individuals and as a global body. We wish you peace.

FORTY

Demystifying the Process of Channeling

Hannah Beaconsfield

Channeling is a perfectly natural phenomenon. Everyone is doing it all the time. It is simply the rising to conscious awareness of information, feelings and impulses that have their source in the broader multidimensional levels of the unconscious.

The multilevel unconscious has access to layers of our subconsciously stored data, such as other life experiences — past, present, future and parallel. This includes data about ourselves as incarnated inhabitants of ET world cultures and as interdimensional beings, such as those who have ascended to lightbodies or angelic energies who resonate with our vibrational family signature. Our vibrational spirit families are a part of the total relatedness of All That Is. Therefore theoretically we have omniscience, or access to all and everything.

Our capacity to bring any of this knowing to our conscious perception and communicate it to others is limited by the level of reality on which we live, our belief systems and our individual abilities as a conduit. The means by which we normally bring this information through on a third-density world is through the filters of inspiration, intuition, imagination, dreaming, creative activities and the life choices we make. Everyone is interacting on nonconscious levels all the time. How much of this information and what type gets through depends on the individual.

Creative artists are literally collaborating with other non-physical creative energies for their inspiration. The same is true in other professions to varying degrees. In the simplest of endeavors like going shopping for a particular item, when we are operating as a clear channel we are intuitively led to the right store to find exactly what we want.

Those who channel at a professional level have laid the groundwork for their work by other lives spent in learning the skills. They then go through a period of learning or self-training to hone the skill for this life.

There are a wide variety of skills that create specialties among those who have particular gifts for channeling. Some are more akin to what used to be called mediums and can contact the recently deceased to exchange messages of comfort for both sides. Some excel at personal readings, having the clairvoyance to assist individuals with personal problems and life choices. Others primarily access information regarding the nature of metaphysics and metapsychology to assist us in broadening our understanding of our reality and our place in the divine plan.

What is the channel experiencing during the channeling process? In the case of full-trance channels, the aware consciousness and the personality willingly step aside so that the spirit/entity can operate and communicate through the body. This is not a form of possession, for there is a mutual agreement by the participating parties and an established trust.

The full-trance channel usually has no recollection of what transpired. This type of channeling can produce dramatic effects like speaking in foreign languages, giving accurate details of historical events and creating changes in the appearance, movement and voice of the channel. Well-known channels like Edgar Cayce, Jane Roberts and J. Z. Knight are different examples of full-trance channels.

The most common type of channel bringing through information today is the semitrance channel. Semitrance channels go into an altered state of consciousness, like a light trance or daydreaming. They have an awareness of what is being said or written but are detached sufficiently to allow information outside their living-plane conscious mind to get through.

In this type of channeling the conduit is a more equal participant in the process than in full-trance channeling. The vocabulary, the stored data, the education and life experiences of the channel are called upon to serve the message. The channel too has an aware participation in that she/he can edit or even censor material she doesn't want to come through. This might simply be due to the channel's sensitivity about what subjects Earth dwellers of that particular culture speak about in public. Or it might be a subject the channel has a personal difficulty with and would prefer the information be brought through another channel.

The most important aspect of this is that the channel participates in the process because semitrance channeling is a bridge of consciousness that will open the way for fully conscious channeling. This will not be just for a selected few, but for the total mass consciousness of all Earth dwellers.

Semitrance channels are laying the groundwork for the expansion of the total population. The current level of natural access to unconscious information will expand to instant access to the universal library. This is also called the akashic records of all knowledge of all things in all time and all space. When will this skill be a natural part of the world consciousness? Maybe a millennium from now, maybe a century or maybe much sooner. The semitrance channels are showing the way, and our world is on a fast track to the future.

As for accommodating the current information coming through, whether you are listening to your own intuitive feelings or reading metaphysical material, there are some things to consider. No matter how simple the message or how complex the material, all must be translated for understanding on the third-dimensional level of conscious understanding. This translation necessarily distorts the information. And each channel colors it with her own feelings and beliefs about reality. This does not invalidate the information, but it can cause confusion when channels speak in diametric opposition to each others' information.

In the present Earth thinking, all information must be tested by reason and found to have a concrete base, or it is without value. With channeled material you are handling a different type of information flow. Channeled material at present comes through right-brain activity. It is downloaded in general concepts, a whole picture or pattern. The channel works in a blended manner to translate the package into a specific explanation. The vocabulary and other stored data from the channel's life experience is used in the translation.

If you listen for the concept — the big picture behind the channeled words — you can absorb the material and pass it through your own translator. This will make the channeling a cocreative process, and you will be using your right brain to grasp the meaning. When you have a better understanding of the process, you can make better use of the information for yourself.

Yes, we all have the capacity to channel information. We all have free access to the universal library of all there is to know. However, not all of us can "read" on the same level or even take interest in reading many of the different subjects. So each uses the library in her own way to serve her own needs. This is true whether we "take out" books ourselves or ask someone else to do the research for us.

As our species moves out of the third-density level of reality, we will all expand our capacity to access the library materials. All individuals will have the ability to channel easily any information they want from the universal library. There will also be much less lost in translation by the expanded levels of consciousness that are even now evolving on our world.

FORTY-ONE

A Fifth Column of Benign Infiltration

Hannah Beaconsfield

It is no longer a case of Earth dwellers expecting or dreading, hoping or fearing that contact with other worlds will occur soon. The number of ET walk-ins and starseeds is reaching a critical mass. "They" are here—and they are *us*.

It is not like the infiltration of an enemy fifth column that has designs for world domination, no matter how many fearful movies give voice to this paranoia. It is the reunion of family members. Other aspects of our spirits, with deep roots in ET world cultures, are projecting into bodies of those who have finished their work on Earth and are willing to allow their bodies to be recycled instead of dying with the spirit's transition. This is in no way an "invasion of the body-snatchers." This is not a hostile takeover, but a benign and practical use of resources.

In addition, there are many parents who on unconscious levels are agreeing to provide a new body for a spirit with high levels of ET experience. These starseeds and walk-ins resonate the vibratory signature of otherworld civilizations. Rather than infiltrators, they are more like ambassadors for their planetary energies. As these energies move among us and within us, we are being prepared to become intergalactic citizens in a subtle, indirect but very effective way.

The next few years will see an influx of walk-ins and starseeds as never before in this world's history. The purpose of such a major "diplomatic mission" is not just to prepare us for open contact by familiarizing us with ET energies, but to provide help, support and guidance for our transformation to the light world and light people we are becoming.

It is not even necessary for the walk-ins and starseeds to be aware of their status as such. With or without conscious knowledge, they will play out their parts as ambassadors. However, sometimes the conscious knowledge helps relieve some of the confusion that can occur when one spirit takes over the life circumstances created by another spirit or helps relieve the sense of alienness many starseeds feel, particularly if they have had no previous lives on Earth.

No one can truly identify walk-ins or starseeds; however, there are psychics who can intuit the probability of an exchange or the presence of an "alien" energy and help these people explore and sense the truth for themselves. When you examine your life situation, it often becomes very clear that a walk-in or starseed situation not only feels right, but is the most logical explanation.

So the ETs have "landed" and are here now. And more and more are coming. Their presence will become so familiar a vibration that when those in their ET bodies and ET craft arrive, the shock will be diffused by those already living among us.

DIRECTORY

I am including a directory of reading material, channels, healers and metaphysical practitioners because I know how much it would have meant to me in 1982 to have had somewhere to turn for guidance and support. I don't want to give any impression that walk-ins are part of some exclusive club. Everyone is, or will be, experiencing very challenging changes as our planetary family moves into expanded dimensions. The directory is made up of many different guidance sources for anyone and everyone who needs help. The names listed here are sources and individuals of whom I have some knowledge and who I believe are valuable. However, just because I feel aligned with them doesn't mean everyone else will. My hope is that the directory will either provide direct help or lead individuals to other sources with whom they do feel aligned. Above and beyond these resources, there is always a multitude of spirit and angelic guides who are available to all of us all of the time.

— Hannah Beaconsfield

Reading Material

✷ *The Seth Material.* This is a series of books by Jane Roberts. These books of channeled material provide basic metaphysical concepts particularly relevant to the late-twentieth-century thinking person. They are from several different publishers and can be found in most metaphysical book stores. *Seth Speaks* and *The Nature of Personal Reality* are metaphysical primers.

✷ The *Sedona Journal of Emergence!* This is a magazine of channeled information from a wide spectrum of channels, including leading metaphysical thinkers. It also includes articles on alternate healing modalities. For subscriptions write to P.O. Box 1526, Sedona, AZ 86339, phone (800) 450-0985 or fax (520) 282-4130.

✷ *Royal Priest Research* releases books and tapes channeled by Lyssa Royal-Holt. Lyssa has created several books concerned with extraterrestrials and preparation for inter-world contact as well a tapes on many metaphysical subjects. For a catalog, send two first-class stamps to P.O. Box 30973, Phoenix, AZ 85046.

✷ *The Isis Connection.* This is a newsletter edited by walk-in Isis. It features articles by nationally known and newly emerging channels. There is also information on UFO sightings from around the world. Send $3 for a sample issue to P.O. Box 1636, Gresham, OR 97030-0521.

✷ *I'm O.K., I'm Just Mutating,* channeled by Zarah of the Golden Star Alliance. This book contains valuable information on the effects of the planetary transformation on our human bodies. Available from Light Technology Publishing, P.O. Box 1526, Sedona, AZ 86339.

✷ *Your Power on a Plate* by Andrew, channeling the Essassani entity Elan. For tapes and books of channeled wisdom from a future extraterrestrial civilization, write InterAction, P.O. Box 332, Milford, CT 06460.

✷ *Bashar: Blueprint for Change* by Darryl Anka. Compiled by Luana Ewing. A message from the future transmitted from an extraterrestrial intelligence. Available from New Solutions Publishing, 20915 NE 77th St., Redmond, WA 98053.

Organizations and Centers

✷ WE International (Walk-ins for Evolution). This is an organization established to assist walk-ins to understand the phenomenon with which they are dealing and to connect with others for mutual support. WE International puts out a quarterly newsletter. For information write to P.O. Box 120633, St. Paul, MN 55112.

✷ Ascension Adjustment. Darla Sims is starting a data base of people who are experiencing the "ascension syndrome." If you are interested in participating in this project designed to give mutual help, send name, address and phone number with a SASE and $1 to defray costs. Darla is also the compiler of the *Directory of New Age and Alternate Publications*. Write P.O. Box 12280, Mill Creek, WA 98082-0280.

✷ **Ascordia Center.** Walk-in Amy Bortner is the director of this center, which serves the Philadelphia area. Named for the angelic entity whom Amy channels, it is a healing center for personal growth and spiritual development. Amy is a certified massage therapist and Reiki healer who also provides spiritual counseling through channeling. Write for information on classes and events to 7904 Germantown Ave., Rear Bldg., Philadelphia, PA 19118.

✷ **Mystical Journey, Ltd.** Two individual practitioners lead transformational travel experiences to sacred sites. These practitioners are Barbara and Manos Angelakis. Barbara is an author, channel and adept of the Atlantean and Egyptian mysteries. Manos does energetic healing and balancing work. He is a shamanic practitioner and teacher of the Arctic traditions. Contact via e-mail at *mysticaljourney@juno.com* or call 1-800-879-6519.

✷ **CSETI** (The Center for the Study of Extraterrestrial Intelligence). This is an organization that, under the direction of Steven Greer, M.D., works to initiate contact with ETs (encounters of the fifth kind). They train investigators in their carefully delineated procedures and are accumulating a great deal of research material. You can contact CSETI at P.O. Box 15401, Asheville, NC 28813.

Metaphysicians and Individual Practitioners

✷ **Elmarilla Bailey** is a channel of an integrated stream of frequencies from the ascended masters and the Great Brotherhood of Light. She provides channeled spiritual guidance, past-life regressions and workshops in channeling. Elmarilla is a certified hypnotherapist, lecturer, author and ordained minister. Contact her at Discoveries Unlimited, P.O. Box 1568, Clarksville, GA 305523.

✷ **Dr. Caron Goode** is a walk-in who has a doctorate in counseling and psychology from George Washington University. She does transpersonal counseling, spiritual readings and mentoring. Contact her at 8075 North 41st St., Longmont, CO 80503. Caron is also affiliated with The International Breath Institute, which provides training in TransformBreathing for personal development and/or professional certification. Address: 2525 Arapahoe Ave., Suite E4-287, Boulder, CO 80302.

✷ **Ed Hager** is a walk-in written about in Ruth Montgomery's *Threshold to Tomorrow* and has been channeling information since 1987 from a group of entities who refer to themselves as the Teachers. Ed corresponds with a multitude of individuals around the globe. He and his wife Mary live in York, Pennsylvania. You can write to him at 11 Crestview Drive, York, PA 17402-4908 or through e-mail at *EHager906@aol.com*.

✷ **Marti Lebow** is a healer using a channeled integrated approach to bodywork through energy balancing. Contact her at C3 Lexington Hill, Harriman, NY 10926.

✷ **Joan Norton**, licensed psychotherapist, and **Sally Norton**, licensed acupuncturist and master herbologist. Soul Attunement Healing for imbalances of body/soul. Joan practices psychology within a spiritual context including multidimensional reality work. Sally heals the body using intuitive guidance from the client's and her own soul plane. Channeling is also available. Contact Joan and Sally at 564 Larchmont Blvd. #102 & 105, Los Angeles, CA 90004.

✷ **Michael Schuster** is a metaphysical speaker and channel who conducts "soul blueprint readings" and past-life regressions. Contact him at Sufra Publications, 1264 Muddy Creek Forks Rd., Airville, PA 17302.

✷ **Bill Tomaszewski** is a walk-in, channel and Reiki practitioner who was trained by Beth Gray. He was the founder and for several years director of a support group for channels in his town. Bill is something of an ambassador and networker for We International and walk-ins in general. He can be contacted at 263 North Main St., New Hope, PA 18938.

Cover Art

Stairway To The Stars

Crystal Visions Fine Art
Huntington Beach, CA 92648
(714) 969-7368

THE EXPLORER RACE SERIES

1 the EXPLORER RACE

This book presents humanity in a new light, as the explorers and problem-solvers of the universe, admired by the other galactic beings for their courage and creativity. Some topics are: **The Genetic Experiment on Earth; The ET in You: Physical Body, Emotion, Thought and Spirit; The Joy, the Glory and the Challenge of Sex; ET Perspectives; The Order: Its Origin and Resolution; Coming of Age in the Fourth Dimension and much more!**

574p $25.00

2 ETs and the EXPLORER RACE

In this book Robert channels Joopah, a Zeta Reticulan now in the ninth dimension, who continues the story of the great experiment — the Explorer Race — from the perspective of his race. The Zetas would have been humanity's future selves had not humanity re-created the past and changed the future.

237p $14.95

3 Origins and the Next 50 Years

Some chapters are: **THE ORIGINS OF EARTH RACES**: Our Creator and Its Creation, The White Race and the Andromedan Linear Mind, The Asian Race, The African Race, The Fairy Race and the Native Peoples of the North, The Australian Aborigines, The Origin of Souls. **THE NEXT 50 YEARS**: The New Corporate Model, The Practice of Feeling, Benevolent Magic, Future Politics, A Visit to the Creator of All Creators. **ORIGINS OF THE CREATOR**: Creating with Core Resonances; Jesus, the Master Teacher; Recent Events in Explorer Race History; On Zoosh, Creator and the Explorer Race. 339p $14.95

THE EXPLORER RACE SERIES

4 EXPLORER RACE: Creators and Friends — the Mechanics of Creation

As we explore the greater reality beyond our planet, our galaxy, our dimension, our creation, we meet prototypes, designers, shapemakers, creators, creators of creators and friends of our Creator, who explain their roles in this creation and their experiences before and beyond this creation. As our awareness expands about the way creation works, our awareness of who we are expands and we realize that a part of ourselves is in that vast creation — and that we are much greater and more magnificent than even science fiction had led us to believe. Join us in the adventure of discovery. It's mind-stretching!

435p $19.95

5 EXPLORER RACE: Particle Personalities

All around you in every moment you are surrounded by the most magical and mystical beings. They are too small for you to see as single individuals, but in groups you know them as the physical matter of your daily life. Particles who might be considered either atoms or portions of atoms consciously view the vast spectrum of reality, yet also have a sense of personal memory like your own linear memory. These particles remember where they have been and what they have done in their infinitely long lives. Some of the particles we hear from are Gold, Mountain Lion, Liquid Light, Uranium, the Great Pyramid's Capstone, This Orb's Boundary, Ice and Ninth-Dimensional Fire. 237p $14.95

THE EXPLORER RACE SERIES

6 EXPLORER RACE: EXPLORER RACE and BEYOND

In our continuing exploration of how creation works, we talk to Creator of Pure Feelings and Thoughts, the Liquid Domain, the Double-Diamond Portal, and the other 93% of the Explorer Race. We revisit the Friends of the Creator to discuss their origin and how they see the beyond; we finally reach the root seeds of the Explorer Race (us!) and find we are from a different source than our Creator and have a different goal; and we end up talking to All That Is! 360p $14.95

7 EXPLORER RACE and ISIS

Isis sets the record straight on her interaction with humans — what she set out to do and what actually happened. $14.95

A EXPLORER RACE: Material Mastery Series

Secret shamanic techniques to heal particular energy points on Earth, which then feeds healing energy back to humans. $14.95

LIGHT TECHNOLOGY PUBLISHING

A BEGINNER'S GUIDE TO THE PATH OF ASCENSION

This volume covers the basics of ascension clearly and completely, from the spiritual hierarchy to the angels and star beings, in Dr. Stone's easy-to-read style. From his background in psychology he offers a unique perspective on such issues as karma, the transcendence of the negative ego, the power of the spoken word and the psychology of ascension.

$14.95 Softcover 166p ISBN 1-891824-02-3

GOLDEN KEYS TO ASCENSION AND HEALING
REVELATIONS OF SAI BABA AND THE ASCENDED MASTERS

This book represents the wisdom of the ascended masters condensed into concise keys that serve as a spiritual guide. These 420 golden keys present the multitude of methods, techniques, affirmations, prayers and insights Dr. Stone has gleaned from his own background in psychology and life conditions and his thorough research of all the ancient and contemporary classics that speak of the path to God realization.

$14.95 Softcover 206p ISBN 1-891824-03-1

MANUAL FOR PLANETARY LEADERSHIP

Here at last is an indispensible book that has been urgently needed in these uncertain times. This book lays out, in an orderly and clear fashion the guidelines for leadership in the world and in one's own life. It serves as a reference manual for moral and spiritual living and offers a vision of a world where strong love and the highest aspirations of humanity triumph.

$14.95 Softcover 284p ISBN 1-891824-05-8

YOUR ASCENSION MISSION
EMBRACING YOUR PUZZLE PIECE

This book shows how each person's puzzle piece is just as vital and necessary as any other. Fourteen chapters explain in detail all aspects of living the fullest expression of your unique individuality.

$14.95 Softcover 248p ISBN 1-891824-09-0

REVELATIONS OF A MELCHIZEDEK INITIATE

Dr. Stone's spiritual autobiography, beginning with his ascension initiation and progression into the 12th initiation, is filled with insight, tools and information. It will lift you into wondrous planetary and cosmic realms.

$14.95 Softcover ISBN 1-891824-10-4

HOW TO TEACH ASCENSION CLASSES

This book serves as an ideal foundation for teaching ascension classes and presenting workshops. The inner-plane ascended masters have guided Dr. Stone to write this book, using his Easy-to-Read-Encyclopedia of the Spiritual Path as a foundation. It covers an entire one- to two-year program of classes.

$14.95 Softcover 136p ISBN 1-891824-15-5

LIGHT TECHNOLOGY PUBLISHING

SHINING THE LIGHT
BEHIND THE SCENES

Channeled by Robert Shapiro and Arthur Fanning

THE TRUTH ABOUT WHAT IS REALLY HAPPENING

Shining the light of truth on the ETs, UFOs, time-travel, alien bases of the Earth, Controllers, the Sinister Secret Government and much more!

SHINING THE LIGHT
The Battle Begins

Revelations about the Secret Government and their connections with ETs. Information about renegade ETs mining the Moon, ancient Pleiadian warships, underground alien bases and many more startling facts.

$12.95 Softcover 208p ISBN 0-929385-66-7

SHINING THE LIGHT II
The Battle Continues

Continuing the story of the Secret Government and alien involvement. Also information about the Photon Belt, cosmic holograms photographed in the sky, a new vortex forming near Sedona, and nefarious mining on sacred Hopi land.

$14.95 Softcover 418p ISBN 0-929385-71-3

SHINING THE LIGHT III
Humanity's Greatest Challenge

The focus shifts from the dastardly deeds of the Secret Government to humanity's role in creation. The Earth receives unprecedented aid from Creator and cosmic councils, who recently lifted us beyond the third dimension to avert a great catastrophe.

$14.95 Softcover 460p ISBN 0-929385-71-3

SHINING THE LIGHT IV
Humanity Gets a Second Chance

Tells of the incredible vehicle traveling with the Hale-Bopp Comet. Four times the size of the Earth and filled with lightbeings. Also covers the Montauk project, the HAARP project and the uncreation of Hitler.

$14.95 Softcover 557p ISBN 0-929385-93-4

NEW!!!
SHINING THE LIGHT V
Humanity Is Going to Make It

Tells of the the latest in the series!
A rocket scientist in Area 51, symbiotic spacecraft engines, SSG downs military planes, the true purpose of the Mayans. Much more including cloning, recent UFO activity, angels, grid lines, Zetas restructuring the past and manifestation powers.

$14.95 Softcover 330p ISBN 1-891824-00-7

LIGHT TECHNOLOGY PUBLISHING

VYWAMUS
JANET MCCLURE

TOOLS FOR TRANSFORMATION

PRELUDE TO ASCENSION

Tools for Transformation

Janet McClure channeling Djwhal Khul, Vywamus & others

Your four bodies, the Tibetan Lesson series, the Twelve Rays, the Cosmic Walk-in and others. All previously unpublished channelings by Janet McClure.

$29.95 Softcover 850p ....ISBN 0-929385-54-3

THE SOURCE ADVENTURE

Life is discovery, and this book is a journey of discovery "to learn, to grow, to recognize the opportunities — to be aware." It asks the big question, "Why are you here?" and leads the reader to examine the most significant questions of a lifetime.

$11.95 Softcover 157p ....ISBN 0-929385-06-3

SCOPES OF DIMENSIONS

Vywamus explains the process of exploring and experiencing the dimensions. He teaches an integrated way to utilize the combined strengths of each dimension. It is a how-to guidebook for living in the multidimensional reality that is our true evolutionary path.

$11.95 Softcover 176p ....ISBN 0-929385-09-8

AHA! The Realization Book (with Lilian Harben)

If you are mirroring your life in a way that is not desirable, this book can help you locate murky areas and make them "suddenly . . . crystal clear." Readers will find it an exciting step-by-step path to changing and evolving their lives.

$11.95 Softcover 120p ....ISBN 0-929385-14-4

SANAT KUMARA Training a Planetary Logos

How was the beauty of this world created? The answer is in the story of Earth's Logos, the great being Sanat Kumara. A journey through his eyes as he learns the real-life lessons of training along the path of mastery.

$11.95 Softcover 179p ....ISBN 0-929385-17-9

LIGHT TECHNIQUES That Trigger Transformation

Expanding the Heart Center . . . Launching your Light . . . Releasing the destructive focus . . . Weaving a Garment of Light . . . Light Alignment & more. A wonderfully effective tool for using light to transcend. Beautiful guidance!

$11.95 Softcover 145p ....ISBN 0-929385-00-4

LIGHT TECHNOLOGY PUBLISHING

more great books!

LYNN BUESS

NUMEROLOGY: NUANCES IN RELATIONSHIPS

The foremost spokesman for numerology and human behavior focuses on relationships. With clear and direct style he identifies the archetypal patterns of each numerical combination. By providing clues to conscious and unconscious issues, Lynn gives the reader choices of behavior in relationships.

$13.75 Softcover 310p

ISBN 0-929385-23-3

NUMEROLOGY FOR THE NEW AGE

An established standard, explicating for contemporary readers the ancient art and science of symbol, cycle, and vibration. Provides insights into the patterns of our personal lives. Includes life and personality numbers.

$11.00 Softcover 262p ISBN 0-929385-31-4

CHILDREN OF LIGHT, CHILDREN OF DENIAL

In his fourth book Lynn calls upon his decades of practice as counselor and psycho-therapist to explore the relationship between karma and the new insights from ACOA/ Co-dependency writings.

$8.95 Softcover 150p

ISBN 0-929385-15-2

DOROTHY ROEDER

THE NEXT DIMENSION IS LOVE

Ranoash

As speaker for a civilization whose species is more advanced, the entity describes the help they offer humanity by clearing the DNA. An exciting vision of our possibilities and future.

$11.95 Softcover 148p

ISBN 0-929385-50-0

REACH FOR US

Your Cosmic Teachers and Friends

Messages from Teachers, Ascended Masters and the Space Command explain the role they play in bringing the Divine Plan to the Earth now!

$14.95 Softcover 204p

ISBN 0-929385-69-1

CRYSTAL CO-CREATORS

A fascinating exploration of 100 forms of crystals, describing specific uses and their purpose, from the spiritual to the cellular, as agents of change. It clarifies the role of crystals in our awakening.

$14.95 Softcover 288p

ISBN 0-929385-40-3

LIGHT TECHNOLOGY PUBLISHING

A DIVISION OF
LIGHT TECHNOLOGY
PUBLISHING

for kids
of all ages!

THE LITTLE ANGEL BOOKS by LEIA STINNETT

A CIRCLE OF ANGELS
A workbook. An in-depth teaching tool with exercises and illustrations throughout.
$18.95 (8.5" x 11")
ISBN 0-929385-87-X

THE 12 UNIVERSAL LAWS
A workbook for all ages. Learning to live the Universal Laws; exercises and illustrations throughout.
$18.95 (8.5" x 11")
ISBN 0-929385-81-0

ALL MY ANGEL FRIENDS
A coloring book and illustrative learning tool about the angels who lovingly watch over us.
$10.95 (8.5" x 11")
ISBN 929385-80-2

WHERE IS GOD?
Story of a child who finds God in himself and teaches others.
$6.95 ISBN 0-929385-90-X

HAPPY FEET
A child's guide to foot reflexology, with pictures to guide. $6.95
ISBN 0-929385-88-8

WHEN THE EARTH WAS NEW
Teaches ways to protect and care for our Earth.
$6.95 ISBN 0-929385-91-8

THE ANGEL TOLD ME TO TELL YOU GOOD-BYE
Near-death experience heals his fear. $6.95
ISBN 0-929385-84-5

COLOR ME ONE
Lessons in competition, sharing and separateness.
$6.95 ISBN 0-929385-82-9

ONE RED ROSE
Explores discrimination, judgment, and the unity of love.
$6.95 ISBN 0-929385-83-7

ANIMAL TALES
Learning about unconditional love, community, patience and change from nature's best teachers, the animals.
$7.95 ISBN 0-929385-96-9

THE BRIDGE BETWEEN TWO WORLDS
Comfort for the "Star Children" on Earth.
$6.95 ISBN 0-929385-85-3

EXPLORING THE CHAKRAS
Ways to balance energy and feel healthy.
$6.95 ISBN 0-929385-86-1

CRYSTALS FOR KIDS
Workbook to teach the care and properties of stones.
$6.95
ISBN 0-929385-92-6

JUST LIGHTEN UP!
Playful tools to help you lighten up and see the humor in all experiences you create.
$9.95 (8.5" x 11")
ISBN 0-929385-64-0

WHO'S AFRAID OF THE DARK?
Fearful Freddie learns to overcome with love.
$6.95 ISBN 0-929385-89-6